D0126186

Mainstreet Ventures

Mainstreet Ventures

# DISTINCTIVE RECIPES

from Distinctive Eateries

Huron River Press

Copyright © 2005

All rights reserved. No part of this book may be reproduced in
any manner without the express written consent of the publisher,
except in the case of brief excerpts in critical reviews and articles.
All inquiries should be addressed to:

Huron River Press
201 South Main Street, Suite 900
Ann Arbor, MI  48104
www.huronriverpress.com

Food Photography: Mark Thomas, Grand Rapids, Michigan
Photography Assistant: Bob Hazen
Food Stylist: Loretta Gorman
Location Photography: Steve Kuzma, Ann Arbor;
    Brian Myers, Florida; Dale Ferrell, West Virginia;
    Mark Thomas, Grand Rapids
Book Design: Savitski Design, Ann Arbor, Michigan

For Mainstreet Ventures:
Ardrianna Anderson
Christine Brownell
Cheryl Hanewich
Lois Welch Keil
Dorothy McLeod
Janet Nacu
Erik Zahler


Printed and bound in Canada.

10   9   8   7   6   5   4   3   2   1


*Library of Congress Cataloging-in-Publication Data*

Pesusich, Simon, 1946-
    Mainstreet ventures : distinctive recipes from distinctive eateries /
Simon Pesusich.
        p. cm.
    Includes index.
    ISBN 1-932399-08-9 (hardcover : alk. paper)
    1.  Cookery.  I. Title.
    TX714.P4622 2005
    641.5--dc22
                        2005009648

## DEDICATION

Chef Simon Pesusich has spent untold hours working to perfect this book. He worked late nights to meet his deadlines, even while we were opening our newest restaurants. His commitment to excellence is a primary reason for any success our company might enjoy.

Chef, Dennis and I talked about dedicating this book and there are many people we'd like to recognize.

First, we must recognize our loyal guests, many of whom patronized us from the very first day. Second, to all of the chefs, managers and employees, past and present, for their dedication and commitment and for all the contributions they have made toward making our restaurants special.

Lastly, we would like to recognize the lasting and ongoing contributions of Deiter Boehm, our retired partner. Through his wisdom and experience, Mainstreet Ventures has grown to our family of restaurants that exist today.

Michael C. Gibbons
*President, Mainstreet Ventures, Inc.*

# CONTENTS

## Steaks & Chops 111

## La Dolce Vita 149

## Wines & Cigars 185

*Appendices*

# Distinctive meals.

Exceptional service. Delightful dining experiences. Each day, we strive to make these the hallmarks of our distinctive eateries. Approximately 1.5 million guests visit The Chop House, The Real Seafood Company, and Gratzi, just to name a few. In all, Mainstreet Ventures operates 16 distinctive restaurants in Michigan, Ohio, West Virginia and Florida.

Mainstreet Ventures partners Chef Simon Pesusich, Michael Gibbons, and Dennis Serras (from left)

"It's so hard to believe it's been 25 years since opening our first restaurant," says President Michael C. Gibbons. "We've been together longer than I've been married," says business partner Dennis Serras. Our lifelong passion for food inspired our restaurants—and this book.

How did we come to start our own restaurant? It's the proverbial response: We thought we could do it better. We left our old jobs and never looked back. At first, we struggled like any small business, sweating bullets, leveraged to the hilt. We learned from our mistakes and moved on.

Today, Mainstreet Ventures consists of three partners: Dennis Serras, Mike Gibbons and Chef Simon Pesusich. That's our corporate team. It's small and lean. Though Dennis might disagree, referring to himself as "the big, fat Greek partner." We work really hard, love what we do, and it reflects in our business. Our restaurants don't exist just so the executives of our company have a place to party. We exist for our restaurants—our clientele who visit, and the people who work here—not the other way around.

**Over the years,** we have created an environment where we attract and keep great people. Some folks have worked with us since we began 25 years ago, which is almost unheard of in the restaurant business. People always ask, 'Where do you get your managers?' We grow them.

Our respect for people shows in our commitment to the communities where our restaurants reside. "When we open a new restaurant, we adopt a charity to support that year. Being part of our community means giving back," says Mike. In 2004, Mainstreet Ventures helped raise over $250,000 for local charitable organizations. We also created a tuition-reimbursement program that contributes over $50,000 to our company's eligible student employees each year, helping them achieve dreams of higher education.

It's clear we enjoy assisting the community with its future and vision. How do we want to be thought of when it comes to future plans for our restaurants? "Gun slingers," Dennis jokingly says. "We're really creative, excel at developing concepts, and want a regional prominence, whether it's the Midwest, or Florida…which is more related than you might think, when you take into consideration a high percentage of current residents are originally from Michigan, Ohio and New York. We understand them," he says with a wink.

Though we may identify with them, we also acknowledge the taste differences of each region. "In Florida, for instance, they don't drink coffee or order much pasta," says Dennis. And even when areas are close in proximity, Chef Simon notes those differences can be significant: "You cannot do certain things in Ann Arbor that you might do in Toledo, even though they're both so close in terms of distance. You have to go, sample the food of the area, talk to people," says Chef Simon. "When we do a menu, we do at least 20 drafts. Chef Simon starts out, then other teams look at it and give their input. We constantly tweak it, " says Mike.

That's true of our latest concept, Carson's, which has a warm and cozy feel.

In terms of the menu, "eclectic contemporary American food," describes it best. Basically, it's a neighborhood restaurant that offers the best comfort food from scratch, like roasted chicken, baby back ribs, sandwiches, and home cooking like fried green tomatoes.

**While we average** opening about two new restaurants a year, there are no plans for franchises. Dennis quickly points out, "It's not like we haven't been approached about it. That's just not our thing. We won't be opening a million restaurants." In some cases, we have more than one location of the same restaurant—for example, The Real Seafood Company in Ann Arbor, Toledo and Naples—but the only similarity is in the name. Each is unique in its own way, from the menu and food presentation to the décor. The cookie cutter is definitely absent from this kitchen.

"The highlight and challenge of Mainstreet Ventures is the variety of our restaurants," says Chef Simon. Each has a different theme, different menu, a different look and a different customer to please. But one thing is consistent throughout. All of our food is made from scratch. I spend a lot of time with suppliers to make sure we get the best ingredients." When asked how quality is maintained, Chef Simon answers, "It's not just my doing. It's our good people. You can develop a recipe and good standards, but in the end, it's up to them to maintain. I cannot take all that credit."

And though Chef Simon is humble when it comes to his influence, his partners are not.

"Our greatest asset is Chef Simon. He does not take short cuts. When helping out during one of our restaurant openings, I tried persuading Chef Simon to get the dish out faster," says Mike.

"Do you want it now, or do you want it right?" was Chef Simon's answer.

"I want it right now," Mike jokingly said.

The Chop House, Ann Arbor

Palio, Ann Arbor

"He's a perfectionist," Mike says about Chef Simon, whether it's developing the recipes in this book or the kitchen, for that matter.

"It's not easy to condense a recipe," says Chef Simon. "First of all, I'm normally cooking for more people. Everything we might automatically do as professional chefs has to be described. I didn't give this to an assistant to do. I've tested every recipe in this book."

We sifted through thousands of recipes and shared the secrets to our most popular menu selections here. For instance, our Parmesan Crusted Sole is included because it's a number-one seller. We sell 300 pounds of flounder in Naples, Florida every week. What's Chef Simon's favorite recipe? As always, Chef Simon answers honestly: "It doesn't make a difference what I like. It's what our guests like. The choices here reflect their favorites."

People like you have made our restaurants a success. For this, we thank you. Take our expertise home and enjoy the satisfaction these recipes will bring to your kitchen.

**The Partners:** Dennis Serras was born in Schenectady, New York into a two-generation restaurant family. He worked from youth through high school learning all aspects of the family business. In 1965, Dennis arrived in the Ann Arbor area to study business. At the time, he worked in operations at local restaurants, hungering to learn all the secrets of running an upscale restaurant. He got plenty of hands-on experience in 1973, when he opened three of Chuck Muer's restaurants in just two years. Around this time, Dennis met Mike Gibbons, who was working at the Charley's Crab in Cincinnati, Ohio. Even after Dennis left, they remained friends. In 1975, he had the opportunity to use his skills in developing his own restaurant, The Real Seafood Company in Ann Arbor.

Mike Gibbons grew up in Charleston, West Virginia and earned his degree

Chef Simon Pesusich (lower right) and the chefs of Mainstreet Ventures

at Xavier University in Cincinnati while working for Charley's Crab. He took a year off after graduation with plans of going to law school, when in 1973 he was transferred to manage the Gandy Dancer in Ann Arbor, Michigan. Mike enjoyed the restaurant business so much, he never went to law school and worked for the Muer Corporation in restaurant management until 1979. When the opportunity came about to join Dennis at Real Seafood, Mike's father, a high profile corporate executive, offered some advice: 'If you can, go do something on your own and be master of your own destiny.' Mike joined forces with Dennis.

In 1981, Dennis and Mike invited former boss Dieter Boehm, who is now retired, to form Mainstreet Ventures. Dieter's vast experience with the restaurant business proved beneficial. The only thing missing from the corporate team was a world-class chef. In 1982, Mainstreet Ventures was complete when Chef Simon Pesusich became their Executive Chef and business partner.

A native of Solina, Croatia, Chef Simon completed his formal training in Pula, Yugoslavia in 1964 and apprenticed in Switzerland and Austria. He began his work experience in North America as Assistant Chef of the Royal Canadian Yacht Club and Sous Chef of the director's private dining room of the Canadian Imperial Bank in Toronto. After coming to the United States, he spent three years in Los Angeles and San Francisco as Sous and Executive Chef. In 1976, he came to metropolitan Detroit, where he worked as Sous Chef at the Hyatt Regency Hotel, served as Executive Chef at the Michigan Inn, the Grosse Pointe Yacht Club and the Hotel Ponchartrain, where he first met Mike Gibbons, the Food and Beverage Director. The synergy created by this fortuitous meeting has been the inspiration for the successive, distinctive eateries of Mainstreet Ventures.

Tidewater Grill, Charleston

Carson's, Fort Myers

Blue Pointe, Fort Myers

# Seafood served simply.

That's our philosophy at Mainstreet Ventures, whether serving Pan Roasted Chilean Sea Bass in one of our upscale seafood restaurants, or something more casual, like Maryland Crab Cakes, in one of our seafood grills.

We use only the freshest fish in our seafood recipes, and we're willing to pay a little extra to get the quality we want. Foley's Seafood Company, on the East Coast, is our primary supplier of premium seafood. We rely on Foley's not only to deliver the top catch from each day's fishing, but also to educate and train our employees about proper handling of this highly perishable product. For example, fish must be kept as cold as possible until they're cooked, so employees are taught to cut and prepare them while they're still in the coolers.

The three Real Seafood Companies — in Ann Arbor, Michigan, Naples, Florida and Toledo, Ohio — offer premium seafood at its best. In the heart of downtown Ann Arbor, we serve favorites like Paella A La Valenciana, a seafood specialty of Spain, or Sautéed Whitefish with dried Michigan cherries, shiitake mushrooms and shallots.

In Toledo, Ohio in a spectacular space on the waterfront, entering guests are greeted by an impressive 10,000-pound ceramic relief cityscape of Toledo, Spain, which sent the sculpture as a gift to its sister city in Ohio. The restaurant's centerpiece is a huge statue of the sea-god Neptune who looks right at home in the massive main dining room, with its 35-foot ceiling. While you are waiting, don't forget to visit the fabulous raw seafood bar.

The Real Seafood in Naples, Florida in an atmosphere that is both elegant and comfortable, features a diverse menu of daily fresh catches, weekly Chef's features and, of course, fresh oysters, in a beautiful setting. Guests particularly like being seated at the large scalloped booths, especially the one that surrounds a nearly 40-foot high preserved palm tree. They also enjoy relaxing outside on the patio.

At our seafood grills, Tidewater Grill, in Charleston, West Virginia and Blue Pointe, in Fort Myers, Florida, we serve a wide variety of fresh fish, pastas,

Tidewater Grill, Charleston

Real Seafood Co., Toledo

Tidewater Grill, Charleston

sandwiches and salads. When we opened Tidewater, which is located in a mall setting, our plan was to serve sandwiches and salads. But this is an example of how we grow and adapt to meet the needs of the surrounding community. People told us they wanted fresh seafood — crab, lobster, shrimp and crab cakes — and they wanted a dinner house, which Charleston was lacking. So we changed the menu and the restaurant became more of a destination point.

The Blue Pointe Oyster Bar and Seafood Grill in Fort Myers features fresh seafood from Florida, Boston and The Great Lakes in a contemporary, open air setting. One of our smaller restaurants, Blue Pointe is located in a busy "lifestyle" mall and attracts a younger crowd. It features a small seafood grill, a major raw seafood bar, and outdoor seating all year around. Chef Simon recommends swordfish in the fall. Swordfish migrate from the south to the north during the spring and summer months, feeding off the rich sea ground and increasing their fat content, which makes them very flavorful.

It takes high standards of quality and freshness, a little extra time and a lot of creativity to serve seafood as it was meant to be served. Take the time to experiment with these delicious recipes. You won't be disappointed.

Real Seafood Co., Naples

Blue Pointe, Fort Meyers

Real Seafood Co., Ann Arbor

## BROILED SEA SCALLOPS *with* SHERRY

Serves 4

1½ lb. sea scallops
3   Tbs. butter, melted
1½ Tbs. sherry wine
1   tsp. sweet paprika
1½ Tbs. chives, chopped
    Salt and pepper to taste

Set the oven to broil.

Remove the elastic ligament attached to scallop. Place scallops into four 8 oz. casserole dishes. Brush the scallops with melted butter. Drizzle sherry wine evenly over top. Sprinkle with salt and pepper and dust with paprika. Clean edges of casseroles with towel.

Place casseroles on baking sheet approximately 3–4 inches under broiler on high heat and broil for 2–3 minutes or until scallops are golden brown and opaque in center. Remove from broiler and brush with remaining butter. Place each casserole on a plate and top with chopped chives.

# CIOPPINO

Cioppino is a seafood stew, an Italian version of French Bouillabaisse.

### Cooking the lobster

4     1¼ lb. live lobsters

Bring a large stockpot of salty water (about 10 quarts) to a boil over high heat. Remove rubberbands. In batches if necessary, place the lobsters in the pot and cover. Cook for about 4 minutes.

Using tongs, transfer the lobster to a work surface. Protecting your hands with a towel twist off the claws and return them to the water to cook for an additional 4 minutes. Meanwhile, working over a bowl to catch the juices, separate the heads from the tails.

Cut the tails off lengthwise. Place the tails in a bowl. When the claws have finished cooking, add to the tails, cover and refrigerate. Using a heavy knife, roughly chop the lobster heads for the stock.

### Cioppino Broth

| | | | |
|---|---|---|---|
| ½ | cup olive oil | 2 | sprigs fresh tarragon |
| | Reserved lobster heads (see above) | ¾ | tsp. sweet paprika |
| 1 | large onion, chopped | ⅛ | tsp. cayenne pepper |
| ½ | cup chopped fennel | ½ | tsp. dried pepper flakes |
| ½ | cup chopped leeks, white part only | 1 | small dried bay leaf |
| 5 | garlic cloves, smashed with knife | 4 | Tbs. tomato paste |
| 4 | 3-inch strips orange zest, removed with vegetable peeler | 1 | cup chopped ripe tomatoes, including juices (use canned tomatoes if ripe are not available) |
| 1 | Tbs. fennel seeds | 1 | cup dry white wine |
| 2 | tsp. ground white pepper | 1 | qt. Chicken Stock (see pg. 147) |
| 10 | sprigs fresh thyme | 1 | Tbs. clam base |
| | | | Coarse salt to taste |

In a large saucepan, heat the olive oil over medium-high heat. Add the chopped lobster heads and cook, stirring occasionally, until the shells are bright red, about 10 minutes. Add the onion, fennel, leeks, and garlic. Reduce the heat to low and cover. Cook the vegetables without coloring until they soften, about 5 minutes.

Add the aromatics and seasoning: the orange zest, fennel seed, white pepper, thyme, tarragon, sweet paprika, cayenne, dried pepper flakes, and bay leaf. Cook for 5–6 minutes to release their perfume. Add the tomato paste, chopped tomatoes, and wine. Raise the heat to high and cook until the wine reduces by half, about 3 minutes.

Add the stock, clam base, and if needed, enough water to cover the ingredients. Season with salt. Bring to boil over high heat. Reduce the heat to low and simmer on low for 45 minutes. Remove from heat and let stand for 20 minutes. Strain through a fine sieve set over a large container. Press hard on solids to extract as much flavor as possible, then discard the solids. If not using immediately, cool to room temperature, cover and refrigerate.

### Assembly

| | | | |
|---|---|---|---|
| 8 | medium fingerling or new potatoes | 16 | large shrimp, unpeeled |
| ¼ | cup olive oil | 16 | littleneck clams, well scrubbed |
| 1 | medium onion, thinly sliced | 32 | mussels, well scrubbed |
| 1 | (about 10 oz.) fennel bulb, thinly sliced | 8 | oz. squid, cleaned, cut cross-wise into ¼-inch thick rings, tentacles reserved |
| 1 | medium red bell pepper, seeded, ribs removed and thinly sliced | 1 | lb. white flaked firm fish (red snapper, grouper, striped bass, etc.), boneless and skinless, cut into 2 oz. pieces |
| 1 | medium yellow bell pepper, seeded, ribs removed and thinly sliced | | Coarse salt and freshly ground pepper |

In a pot of boiling salted water, cook the potatoes until they are tender when pierced with the tip of a knife, 10–15 minutes. Set the potatoes aside in their cooking liquid.

In a large stock pot, heat the oil over medium heat. Add the onion and fennel and cook gently without covering for 4–5 minutes. Add the red and yellow peppers. Continue cooking gently until the vegetables soften, about 15 minutes. The vegetable mixture can be prepared up to 2 hours ahead and kept at room temperature.

Add the strained Cioppino broth and bring to boil over high heat. Drain the potatoes and add to the broth along with the shrimp, clams, fish and mussels. Cover and cook for 3 minutes. Add the cooked lobster with its juices, squid and vegetables. Taste and season with salt and pepper, if necessary. Cook until all the shellfish open, about 3 more minutes. Serve in large, deep soup bowls with crusty bread for dipping in broth.

## HONEY BARBECUED SALMON

Serves 4

1½    lb. salmon filet, boneless and skinless
1½    cup Honey Barbecue Sauce
      Salt and pepper to taste

Preheat oven to 450 degrees.

Cut the salmon filet into 4 equal pieces. Place parchment paper on a 9x12 inch baking
   sheet pan. Brush both sides of each salmon piece with barbecue sauce. Season with
   salt and pepper. Bake in oven for 6 minutes, then switch oven dial to broil and cook
   salmon for 3 more minutes until salmon just flakes. Brush lightly with sauce prior to
   serving. Transfer the salmon onto plates and serve with more of the sauce if you desire.

## HONEY BARBEQUE SAUCE

Serves 2

| | | | |
|---|---|---|---|
| 1 | cup ketchup | 1 | Tbs. curry powder |
| 1 | cup honey | 1 | tsp. sweet paprika |
| ¼ | cup coarse-grained mustard | 1 | tsp. soy sauce |
| ¼ | cup jalapeno pepper, minced | 2 | garlic cloves, minced |
| | (wear rubber gloves) | 1 | Tbs. vegetable oil |
| 2 | Tbs. rice vinegar | ½ | tsp. Worcestershire sauce |
| ½ | tsp. Tabasco | 1 | tsp. lemon juice |
| 3 | Tbs. light brown sugar | ¼ | tsp. ground black pepper |

In a heavy saucepan, stir together sauce and dry ingredients. Bring to boil and simmer,
   stirring occasionally, about 15 minutes. Strain the sauce through a fine sieve. Sauce will
   keep for one week covered and chilled.

# LINGUINE *with* CLAMS

½   cup extra virgin olive oil
⅓   cup chopped fresh parsley leaf
4   large garlic cloves, mashed to a
     paste with a sprinkle of coarse salt
1   cup dry white wine

½   tsp. coarsely cracked black pepper
¼   tsp. crushed red pepper flakes
4   Tbs. canola oil
3   dz. little neck clams, well scrubbed
3   Tbs. unsalted butter
1   lb. dried linguine

In a small bowl, mix the olive oil, parsley, garlic, black and red peppers. Set aside.

In a large saucepan, heat the canola oil over high heat until very hot but not smoking. Add the clams and white wine and cover. Cook for 3–4 minutes, until some of the clams have opened and released their juices. Add the oil mixture and butter. Cover and cook until all the clams open, about 4 minutes. Discard any clams that don't open.

Meanwhile, cook the linguine in a large pot of salted water over high heat until al dente, 8–10 minutes. Drain and use tongs to transfer the pasta and clams to individual bowls. Then spoon the clam broth over all.

## JUMBO SHRIMP COCKTAIL                          Serves 4

The popularity of shrimp cocktail, fried shrimp, and scampi, and the versatility that this
shellfish brings to so many other dishes have made it a staple in American Seafood
Cuisine. Shrimp are usually sold in the fish market without the heads, and in their paper-
thin shells. Sizes of shrimp range from small to jumbo. How you plan to use the shrimp
will determine the size you buy. Jumbo shrimp are particularly impressive and attractive
for a shrimp cocktail.

| | | | |
|---|---|---|---|
| 1½ | lb. shrimp (10–15 shrimp in a pound) | 1 | rib celery, coarsely chopped |
| 1 | cup Cocktail Sauce | 1 | Tbs. peppercorn |
| 2 | lemons (1 whole, 1 cut into wedges) | 2 | bay leaves |
| 1 | Tbs. salt | 2 | qts. water |
| ½ | cup onion, coarsely chopped | | |

### To cook shrimp

In a large saucepan, add water, salt, onion, celery, peppercorn, and bay leaves. Cut 1 lemon
in half and squeeze juice into the saucepan. Bring to a boil. Drop shrimp into rapidly boiling water and stir. Be sure the shrimp are completely covered with water. Cook shrimp for
3–4 minutes, until just pink and tender. Don't overcook. Drain and add shrimp into ice
water immediately to stop the process of cooking. After several minutes drain the shrimp.

### To clean cooked shrimp

Slit the shrimp down the back with a sharp knife, and peel off the shell, leaving the tail shell
on. Carefully pick out the black vein of the back with the tip of your knife. Rinse under
cold water. Shrimp is ready to prepare for your recipe.

Arrange shrimp on a bowl of crushed ice, or simply on a plate or platter. Serve with lemon
wedges and cocktail sauce.

## COCKTAIL SAUCE                              Makes 2 Cups

| | |
|---|---|
| ¾ | cup tomato ketchup |
| ¾ | cup chili sauce |
| ¼ | cup prepared horseradish |
| 2 | tsp. Worcestershire sauce |
| | Juice of one small lemon |
| | Dash of Tabasco sauce |
| | Salt and freshly ground pepper to taste |

In a mixing bowl combine all ingredients and mix well. Refrigerate in a tightly covered
container up to two weeks or until ready to serve.

# LOBSTER BISQUE

| | | | |
|---|---|---|---|
| 1 | lb. live lobster | 1 | Tbs. sweet paprika |
| 5 | Tbs. butter | 2½ | qts. water |
| 1 | fennel bulb, coarsely chopped | 1 | bay leaf |
| 1½ | celery ribs, coarsely chopped | 3 | Tbs. lobster base |
| 2 | carrots, coarsely chopped | 3-4 | fresh thyme sprigs |
| 1 | leek, white part only, coarsely chopped, washed and drained | 3 | cups heavy cream |
| 4 | cloves garlic, minced | ⅓ | cup dry sherry wine, preferably Christian Brothers |
| ⅓ | cup brandy | 1 | tsp. salt, or to taste |
| 2 | Tbs. tomato paste | ½ | tsp. ground white pepper, or to taste |
| | | 1 | Tbs. fresh chives, finely chopped |

Prepare the roux.

In a stock pot, bring water to a boil, twist the claws and tails from the lobster and set aside the bodies. Remove the rubber bands from the claws. Add the claws and tails to the boiling water. Simmer the tails until just cooked, about 4 minutes, and the claws until they turn bright red all over, about 8 minutes. Remove claws and tails to cool and reserve the cooking liquid. Crack the claws, remove the meat from the claws and the tails, cut the meat into small pieces. Cover and refrigerate.

Twist the legs from the lobster bodies and cut the body into large pieces.

Melt the butter in a large saucepan. Add the fennel, celery, carrots, onion, leeks, and garlic and cook over medium heat, stirring frequently, until the vegetables are slightly browned (about 10 minutes).

Add the lobster legs and body pieces and cook over high heat until the shells start to brown, about 8 minutes. Deglaze with brandy.

Add paprika and tomato paste, sauté 3–4 minutes. Stir in the thyme, bay leaves, lobster base and the reserved lobster cooking liquid.

Bring to a boil and simmer for 30 minutes.

Strain through a large sieve pressing on the solids to extract as much liquid as possible.

Bring back to a boil. Whisk in the roux. Season with salt and pepper and stir well. Strain through a fine sieve.

Add the heavy cream and sherry wine and simmer for 10 minutes.

Divide the chopped lobster meat between warmed soup bowls and ladle the soup into the bowls, sprinkling each serving with chives.

## Making the roux
½   lb. butter
½   lb. flour

Melt the butter in a small, heavy saucepan. Whisk in flour and cook the roux over medium heat, stirring often for 10 minutes or until it resembles the color of peanut butter. Let it cool before using for soup.

## MARYLAND-STYLE CRAB CAKES

Mustard Sauce can be prepared one day in advance, covered and refrigerated.

1    cup mayonnaise
¼    cup Dijon mustard
½    lemon fresh squeezed lemon juice
⅓    cup heavy cream

Whip the heavy cream to a soft peak. In a mixing bowl, combine the mayonnaise, Dijon
mustard, dry mustard, lemon juice and whisk well. Fold in the whipped cream until
well combined.

### To make cakes

| | | | |
|---|---|---|---|
| 1 | lb. jumbo lump crab meat | 1 | Tbs. chopped parsley |
| ½ | cup Panko, Japanese style bread crumbs | 2 | tsp. Worcestershire sauce |
| | | 1 | tsp. Dijon mustard |
| 1 | egg | 1 | tsp. salt |
| ¼ | cup + 1 Tbs. mayonnaise | ¼ | tsp. ground black pepper |
| | | 2 | Tbs. canola oil |

In a mixing bowl, combine egg, mayonnaise, Worcestershire sauce, Dijon mustard,
parsley, salt, and pepper and mix well. Add in the breads crumbs and mix once again.
Add the crab meat to the mixture and fold in lightly but thoroughly using a spatula, be
sure not to break up the crab meat. Let the mixture stand in the refrigerator for ½ hour.

Form the crab mixture into balls and place between your palms to make a small patty,
about 2–3 inches in diameter and ½-inch thick.

Heat canola oil in a non-stick sauté pan over medium heat. Add the cakes to the pan in
batches and cook approximately 3–4 minutes on each side until nicely browned.

### Service and Assembly

2    cups mixed baby greens
¼    cup walnuts, toasted
¼    cup pecans, toasted
½    cup strawberries, cut in half
½    cup raspberries
2    Tbs. chives, chopped

Divide baby greens among plates. Add berries over greens and sprinkle with toasted
walnuts and pecans.

Arrange the crab cakes on the greens and spoon with Mustard Sauce. Sprinkle with
chopped chives.

# OYSTER FLORENTINE

18  Blue Point, or any other North
    East cold water oyster, shucked
⅓  lb. sliced bacon, cut into very
    small pieces
½  cup onions, finely diced
2  garlic cloves, minced

1  lb. chopped spinach. If frozen,
    thaw and squeeze out water
½  cup Parmesan and
    fontina cheeses, shredded
¼  cup sherry wine
2  Tbs. butter
2  Tbs. olive oil
    Salt and pepper to taste

Heat the butter and oil in a sauce pan over medium high heat. Add the bacon and sauté until
the bacon is crisp but not burned. Add onions and garlic and cook until soft, translucent.
Add the spinach and continue to cook for two more minutes or until spinach is well heated.
Deglaze with sherry wine and cook until wine is evaporated. Remove from heat and season
with salt and pepper. Let the mixture cool at room temperature.

Using an oyster knife, open the oysters. Cut the muscle on both sides. Leave the meat
on the deeper side of shells. Cover the oyster well with spinach mixture and sprinkle
with cheese.

Place the oysters on a baking sheet and bake in a preheated oven at 400 degrees for
10 minutes or until cheese is completely melted. Remove from oven and serve.

## PAELLA A LA VALENCIANA

Serves 4

*(pay-ell-ya a la val-en ci-ana)*

Paella is undoubtedly the one dish that has become an international classic. The ingredients change for each section of Spain, and indeed almost every family has its one favorite way of preparing this dish. It is by no means a difficult dish to prepare, but it does take time and the proper ingredients.

Natural rice must be used in order to give the necessary flavor to the other ingredients. Saffron, the most expensive coloring in the world, is a must. Good olive oil is necessary also.

It is also a good plan to purchase a Paellera, the special dish used only to make paella. This is a shallow iron pan with sloping sides and two side handles. However, if you wish, a shallow frying pan with sloping sides may be used.

All the ingredients for the paella may be prepared beforehand, except of course for the rice, so really it only takes the time required to cook the rice for the paella to be ready for the table, about 20 minutes.

The Paella from Valencia is famous and is made from a mixture which includes seafood, chicken, pork and sometimes pork sausage. For variety, you can experiment with any other ingredients you prefer. This is our version.

| | | | |
|---|---|---|---|
| 2 | 6 oz. breast of chicken, boneless and skinless | 3 | scallions, chopped |
| ¾ | lb. chorizo sausage links | 2 | Tbs. cilantro, coarsely chopped |
| ⅓ | cup olive oil | ½ | cup green beans, cut finely |
| 1 | cup onion, finely chopped | ½ | cup shelled green peas |
| 2 | cloves garlic, minced | 1½ | cups rice |
| 1 | cup mushrooms, sliced | 3 | cups boiling Chicken Stock (see pg. 147) |
| 2 | ripe tomatoes, peeled, seeded and chopped | 18 | saffron threads |
| | | | Pinch of cayenne |
| 1 | red bell pepper, seeded, ribs removed, cut into fine strips | 8 | large shrimp |
| | | 16 | mussels, scrubbed |
| | | 12 | little neck clams, scrubbed |
| | | | Coarse salt to taste |

Preheat oven to 400 degrees.

Cut the chicken breast into small pieces, season with salt and set aside. In a large sauce pan, bake chorizo sausage in oven for 15–20 minutes. Remove the pan from oven and set aside for 15 minutes to allow the sausage to release their own juices. Remove the chorizo sausage and set aside. In the same saucepan, heat the oil over high heat. Brown the chicken over this heat for 4–5 minutes. Remove the chicken and set aside.

Add the onion and garlic and sauté until translucent. Then add the mushrooms and continue to cook until softened. Add the tomatoes, red peppers, scallions, cilantro and salt and sauté until tender, about 4–5 minutes. Slice the chorizo sausage and mix with vegetables along with chicken, shelled green peas and green beans. Remove the pan from the stove and mix in the cayenne.

Return the pan to the stove. Add in rice and fry until the rice has taken on some color. Meanwhile, heat the chicken stock to boiling. Mix in saffron. Add the Chicken Stock and saffron mixture to the pan and stir well. Bring to boil. Cover and place in oven. Cook for 10 minutes, then add the shrimp, mussels, and clams, and bury them under the cooking rice. Cover again and return to oven for additional 10 minutes. When all is cooked, remove the dish from oven and let stand for 6–8 minutes so that the juices may blend with the rice.

# DOVER SOLE MEUNIERE *or* AMANDINE

4    24–28 oz. each, Dover sole, whole
½    cup all-purpose flour
⅔    cup olive oil

Coarse salt and pepper to taste
Meuniere or Amadine Sauce
1    lemon, cut into wedges, optional

### Meuniere Sauce

⅔    cup dry white wine
1    stick (8 Tbs.) unsalted butter, cold, cut into pieces
⅓    cup lemon juice
4    Tbs. chopped parsley
     Salt and pepper to taste

### Amadine Sauce

1    stick (8 Tbs.) unsalted butter
1    cup sliced, blanched almonds
⅓    cup lemon juice
4    Tbs. chopped parsley
     Salt and pepper to taste

### Skinning and filleting fish

Lay the fish dark side up on a cutting board with the tail toward you. Grasp the fish by the tail end and hold it tightly. Cut through the skin about ½ inch from the tail end. Turn the knife flat against the skin and slide the blade forward until the meat and skin have been separated about 1 inch. Grasp the tail with one hand and with another hard pull take the skin off. Turn the fish over to the white side and repeat process.

Using a sharp knife cut from the head to the tail both dorsal and ventral fins all the way to the flesh. Start on the top (dark) side, cut the center backbone down from head to tail. Turn the knife flat using the spine as a guide, cut toward one periphery, the length of the fish from head to tail leaving it barely attached. Cut the head off.

### Cooking the fish

Preheat the oven to 400 degrees.

Heat the oil in a large 12-inch skillet over medium-high heat. Season the sole with salt and pepper on both sides and dredge in flour. Sauté to a golden brown on both sides, remove fish to broiler pan and cook in 350 degree oven to finish off the sole for about 5–6 minutes. Transfer the sole to a platter and spoon the sauce over the sole. Garnish with lemon.

### To make Meuniere Sauce

Meantime, add white wine to a 10-inch skillet and reduce to half. Add lemon juice and butter a little bit at a time, whisking constantly until all of the butter is incorporated. Stir in parsley, salt and pepper.

### To Make Amandine Sauce

Toast the almonds in an oven for 5–6 minutes or until nicely browned.

Heat a 10 inch sauté pan over moderately high heat. Add in butter, making sure that it does not burn. Stir in lemon juice, toasted almonds, parsley, salt and pepper.

# PAN ROASTED CHILEAN SEA BASS

Serves 4

### For the Bouillabaisse Sauce

| | | | | |
|---|---|---|---|---|
| 1 | large fennel bulb, chopped | | 1 | tsp. white peppercorns |
| 4 | celery stalks, chopped | | 1 | bay leaf |
| 1 | leek, chopped washed and drained | | 3 | sprigs thyme |
| 1 | medium onion, peeled and chopped | | 2 | cups olive oil |
| 3 | cloves garlic, peeled and sliced | | 3 | plum tomatoes, diced |
| 2 | Tbs. fennel seeds | | 3 | cups fish stock |
| 4 | saffron threads | | 3 | cups Chicken Stock (see pg. 147) |
| 1½ | Tbs. sweet paprika | | ⅔ | cup Pernod liquor |
| | | | | Coarse salt and white pepper to taste |

### For the potatoes

8  Yukon Gold potatoes, peeled and quartered
6  saffron threads
   Coarse salt to taste

### For the vegetables

| | | | | |
|---|---|---|---|---|
| 2 | Tbs. unsalted butter | | 1 | large tomato, peeled, seeded and diced |
| 1 | large leek, trimmed and thinly sliced, washed and drained | | 1 | tsp. chopped chives |
| 1 | large fennel bulb, thinly sliced | | 1 | tsp. chopped parsley |
| 2 | Tbs. Fish or Chicken Stock (see pg. 147) | | 1 | tsp. chopped tarragon |
| | | | | Coarse salt and pepper to taste |

### For the sea bass

2  Tbs. olive oil
¼  cup flour
4  6 oz. Chilean sea bass fillets, skinless and boneless
   Coarse salt and pepper to taste

**For the bouillabaisse sauce:** in a large bowl, combine the fennel, celery, leeks, onion, garlic, fennel seeds, saffron, paprika, peppercorns, bay leaf, thyme, and olive oil and toss to combine. Cover with plastic wrap and set aside in the refrigerator to marinate overnight.

To finish the bouillabaisse sauce, strain the marinade thoroughly through a fine mesh sieve, reserving the vegetables and olive oil separately. Heat a large saucepan over medium heat. Place the reserved vegetables in the pan and sauté until translucent. Add the tomatoes and sauté until soft, about 5 minutes.

Add the fish stock, Chicken Stock and Pernod and simmer until almost dry, about 30 minutes. Whisk in the reserved oil and remove from the heat. Strain through a fine mesh sieve, pressing to extract any excess liquid, and discard the vegetables.

Transfer to a medium saucepan and reserve, keeping warm.

**For the potatoes:** in a saucepan, cover the potatoes and saffron with water and bring to a boil. Reduce the heat and simmer until tender, about 15 minutes. Remove from heat and strain. Transfer to a bowl, season and set aside, keeping warm.

**For the vegetables:** in a medium saucepan, melt the butter over medium heat. Add the leeks and fennel and sauté until translucent. Add the fish stock and simmer until tender, about 5 minutes. Add the tomatoes and herbs and sauté until tender, about 3 minutes. Remove from heat, season and set aside keeping warm.

**For the sea bass:** in a medium sauté pan, heat the oil over medium heat. Season, dust the sea bass fillets with flour, and sear on both sides until nicely browned and desired doneness. Remove from heat and set aside, keeping warm.

To finish the sauce, using a hand held immersion blender, blend the bouillabaisse sauce until thick and well combined. Season and set aside keeping warm.

To serve, place the vegetables in the center of large bowls. Set a sea bass fillet and some potatoes around the vegetables and spoon some bouillabaisse sauce around the dish.

## PARMESAN CRUSTED SOLE
## *with* CAPER BEURRE BLANC

Serves 4

1¼ lb. lemon sole filet, boneless and skinless (approximately 5 oz each)
½ cup Panko bread crumbs
1 cup parmesan cheese, shredded
¼ cup flour
1 egg
¼ cup milk
1 tsp. salt
¼ tsp. ground pepper
⅓ cup canola oil
1 cup Caper Beurre Blanc Sauce

In a large mixing bowl, combine bread crumbs, parmesan cheese and flour. In a separate bowl, beat the egg and milk. Season the lemon sole with salt and pepper. Dredge the sole in flour and shake excess of flour off. Dip in egg wash and then into parmesan mixture to coat both sides of filets.

In a large non-stick sauté pan, add the canola oil and heat over medium heat. Add the sole to the skillet and cook for two minutes on each side or until nicely brown. If the fish is not totally cooked, place in a preheated oven at 400 degrees for 2–3 minutes. Divide the fish among four plates and serve with Caper Beurre Blanc Sauce.

## BEURRE BLANC SAUCE

Makes 1 Cup

The foundation for many of my sauces is this wonderfully adaptable sauce, otherwise known as white butter sauce.

½ cup dry white wine
2 tsp. white wine vinegar
2 tsp. fresh lemon juice
2 Tbs. shallots, minced
2 Tbs. heavy cream
½ cup unsalted butter, cut in small pieces
¼ tsp. coarse salt
1 Tbs. capers, drained (optional)
Freshly ground white pepper to taste

Combine wine, vinegar, lemon juice, and shallots in a sauce pan and bring to a boil over medium-high heat. Reduce the liquid, until it becomes syrupy. Add the cream and reduce by half. Turn the heat to low, and add one piece of butter at a time, whipping with a whisk until it is totally incorporated before adding the next piece. Repeat until all the butter is incorporated into the sauce. Be careful not to let the mixture boil, or it will break and separate.

Note: The butter should not melt but should be beaten in, otherwise the sauce will have an oily film to it.

Season with salt and pepper and strain through a fine sieve. Transfer to a double-boiler and keep warm–140 degrees. Watch the temperature because excessive heat will break the sauce.

Variation: At this point you may add drained capers to the sauce (Caper Beurre Blanc for Parmesan Sole) or chopped fresh chives to simplify the dish or to accommodate your own personal taste.

## SALT *and* PEPPER TUNA                    Serves 4

| | |
|---|---|
| ¾ lb. yellowfin tuna loin, no skin or bloodline, cut 3 x 3 x 2¼ | ¼ cup carrots, cut into a fine julienne |
| 1 Tbs. canola oil | ¼ cup scallion, green only, cut into a fine julienne |
| 1½ cup cooked Sushi Rice (see pg. 60) | 1 Tbs. white and black sesame seeds lightly toasted |
| ½ cup Spicy Ponzu Sauce, see recipe below | 1 Tbs. kosher salt |
| 4 Tbs. Wasabi Sauce (see pg. 122) | 2 tsp. black pepper, coarsely ground |
| ½ cup Mango and Pineapple salsa | 1 Tbs. canola oil |

Season tuna loin on all sides with salt and pepper.

Heat a non-stick pan over medium high heat. Add the canola oil, when the oil is smoky, add the tuna, using tongs so as not to burn yourself. Sear the tuna on one side momentarily and repeat on all sides. Remove tuna from pan and set aside. When cool, cover tuna and refrigerate for at least 30 minutes. You may prepare one day in advance.

Arrange four plates, dip sushi mold (3 oz. small ramekins) in cold water and fill with sushi rice, pressing with a spoon to make it level with the rim. Invert the mold onto the center of plates.

Slice the tuna into 12 thin slices and place 3 slices around each sushi mold. Add a small amount of mango and pineapple salsa between each slice. Spoon the Ponzu sauce over the tuna and sprinkle entire plate with toasted sesame seeds. Top the sushi mold with carrots and scallions. Spoon Wasabi sauce around tuna slices.

## MANGO *and* PINEAPPLE SALSA           Makes 2½ Cups

- 1 cup pineapple, peeled, cored and finely diced
- 1 cup ripe firm mango, peeled, pitted and finely diced
- 2 Tbs. red onion, finely diced
- ¼ cup fresh cilantro, chopped
- 1 Tbs. fresh ginger, peeled and minced
- 1 jalapeno chile, seeded and minced
  Juice of two limes or 2 Tbs. fresh passion fruit juice

Combine all the ingredients in a mixing bowl. Chill before serving.

## PONZU SAUCE                              Makes 1 Cup

- 1 cup Mirin (sweet rice wine)
- ¾ cup light soy sauce
- 1 tsp. Sambal (chile sauce/paste), or dried chile flakes, or to taste
- 2 Tbs. fresh lemon juice

Bring the Mirin to a boil in a saucepan, and reduce to ⅓ cup, about 5 minutes. Remove from heat and allow to cool. Whisk in the soy sauce, chile flakes, and lemon juice. Cool to room temperature.

# SAUTEED WHITEFISH
## *with* MICHIGAN DRIED CHERRIES

2   lb. whitefish filet, boneless
    (approx. 4 filets, halved crosswise)
1   cup shiitake mushrooms,
    stems removed, sliced
½   cup Michigan dried cherries
2   Tbs. shallots, finely chopped

⅓   cup dry white wine
½   cup Chicken Stock (see pg. 147)
⅓   cup canola oil
3   Tbs. flour
4   Tbs. butter, room temperature
¼   cup fresh basil, cut into fine strips
    Salt and pepper to taste

Heat the oil in a sauté pan over medium-moderate heat. Season the whitefish with salt and pepper and dust in flour. Shake off excess flour.

Place the whitefish (flesh side down first) into a pan and sauté for approximately 2–3 minutes or until nicely browned. Turn it over and cook for an additional 2–3 minutes. Remove the fish and place on plates. Keep warm.

Add the shiitake mushrooms and shallots and sauté until soft. Deglaze the pan with white wine, add Chicken Stock and cherries. Bring to a boil and simmer for just a few seconds. Add basil and whisk in butter to combine. Season with salt and pepper to taste. Pour the sauce over the fish evenly.

# OYSTERS ROCKEFELLER

For spinach mixture

| | |
|---|---|
| 1 Tbs. unsalted butter | 10 oz. frozen chopped spinach, |
| 1 Tbs. shallots, finely chopped | defrosted and drained well |
| 1 Tbs. scallions, minced | 1 Tbs. Pernod liquor |
| 2 Tbs. chopped parsley | Coarse salt and pepper to taste |

For bechamel sauce

3   Tbs. unsalted butter
3   Tbs. flour, all-purpose
1½  cup milk
    Pinch cayenne pepper
    Coarse salt and pepper to taste

For oysters

1   dz. large Blue Pointe or any other cold water oyster,
        scrubbed, opened, all in the half shell
2   pie or cake tins, half filled with rock salt
1½  cup Hollandaise Sauce (see recipe opposite)

## Bechamel Sauce

Melt butter in a sauce pan.

Stir in flour and cook, stirring 3 minutes without browning. This cooks the flour so sauce will not taste starchy.

Add hot milk all at once and beat sauce with a wire whisk, cooking over moderate heat until sauce is smooth and thickened. Simmer it slowly for 5 minutes then season with salt and pepper. Set aside.

## Spinach Mixture

Melt butter in a sauté pan. Add shallots and scallions and cook briefly or until onions are soft.

Combine spinach, scallions, shallots, parsley, salt and pepper and Pernod in a food processor and puree.

Pour the spinach mixture into béchamel sauce and stir well. Set aside.

## Baking the Oysters

Preheat oven to 400 degrees. Arrange and level oysters on a rock salt bed. Top each oyster with about 2 Tbs. full of spinach mixture. Bake them for about 8 minutes. Top each oyster with about 1 Tbs. of hollandaise sauce and put under broiler to brown lightly. Do not burn. You have to watch it. Transfer the oysters to a large platter using tongs.

## HOLLANDAISE SAUCE

Makes 1½ Cups

4   large egg yolks
2   Tbs. fresh lemon juice
8   oz. (2 sticks) unsalted butter
    Salt and ground white pepper to taste

Remove eggs from refrigerator and let stand for about an hour until they are room
temperature. Separate, and set whites aside for another use.

In a small, heavy saucepan, melt the butter, but don't let it brown. Set butter aside and
keep it warm.

Put egg yolks, lemon juice and 2 Tbs. of water into a stainless mixing bowl and place
over simmering water. Don't let the mixing bowl touch the water below. Whisk egg yolks
briskly until they begin to get thick and creamy.

Remove from heat. Start adding the butter, a drop at a time at first, then in a fine stream,
whisking constantly. Season with salt and pepper.

Keep mixture warm and creamy by placing over warm water at same temperature as
the sauce.

Note: Do not use aluminum utensils because eggs will discolor. Don't try to reheat
hollandaise; if sauce should curdle, beat another egg yolk and gradually whisk the
curdled mixture into fresh egg yolk.

## CALAMARI SAUTEED *with* BANANA *and* CHERRY PEPPERS

Serves 4–6

1   lb. calamari tubes,
      sliced into ¼ inch tick rings
6   cherry peppers, seeded and cut
      into fine strips
3   banana peppers, seeded and cut
      into fine strips

1   Tbs. garlic, minced
4   scallions, chopped
2   Tbs. flat parsley, finely chopped
3   cups canola oil
1½  cups frying batter mix
2   Tbs. olive oil
      Salt and pepper to taste

In a large, deep frying pan, heat canola oil over high heat until temperature reaches about 350 degrees. Dredge the calamari rings into dry batter mix and shake off excess.

Add the calamari to hot oil and stir with metal spoon. Do not crowd the pan. You may have to fry in a few batches. Fry until calamari are crispy and golden, about 30–40 seconds (do not overcook, it will taste rubbery). With a large slotted spoon, transfer the calamari to paper towel. Keep warm.

Meanwhile, heat the olive oil in a large frying pan over medium-high heat. Add the peppers, scallions and garlic and sauté for 2–3 minutes or until tender. Toss in the fried calamari and chopped parsley. Season with salt and pepper. Transfer the calamari to serving platter.

**Note:** Be careful when cutting hot peppers. Use disposable gloves.

## SEAFOOD SALAD

| | | | |
|---|---|---|---|
| 1 | head green romaine lettuce, rinsed and dried | ½ | lb. jumbo shrimp, peeled and deveined |
| 3 | qts. mixed baby greens | ⅓ | lb. calamari, sliced into rings |
| 8 | asparagus, blanched | 1¼ | lb. lobster |
| 8 | red teardrop tomatoes | 1 | cup Basil-Parmesan Vinaigrette |
| 8 | yellow teardrop tomatoes | ½ | cup dry white wine |
| 8 | artichoke hearts | 1 | shallot, chopped |
| ⅓ | lb. sea scallops | ½ | tsp. salt |

Cook lobster in boiling water for 7–8 minutes. Remove from water and let it cool. Crack the tail and claws and reserve the meat.

### Poaching seafood

In a small saucepan, add white wine, 1 cup of water, shallot and salt. Bring to boil. Add in shrimp and shallots and cook for 2 minutes or until shrimp are just pink; then add calamari and cook for 30 seconds or until tender. Drain the seafood. Toss with 2 Tbs. of vinaigrette. Set aside.

### Making the salad

In a large salad bowl, toss the romaine and baby greens with dressing. Divide the tossed greens evenly among four plates. Split the lobster tail in half lengthwise and carefully, with the tip of your knife, pick the black vein out of the back. Rinse with cold water. Cut the claws and tail in half crosswise. Arrange the lobster meat, shrimp, scallops and calamari and remaining ingredients over the greens in a decorative fashion.

## BASIL-PARMESAN VINAIGRETTE

| | | | |
|---|---|---|---|
| 1 | cup fresh basil leaves, packed | ¼ | cup Dijon mustard |
| 2 | Tbs. shallots, sliced | 1½ | cups olive oil |
| 1 | Tbs. garlic, minced | ½ | cup Parmesan cheese, grated |
| ½ | cup white wine vinegar | | Coarse salt and ground black pepper to taste |

In a food processor, add basil, shallots, garlic, vinegar and mustard. Process briefly in 3 or 4 short bursts. Add oil, salt, pepper and cheese. Process in 2 short bursts just to combine. Keep refrigerated up to 1 week.

## STUFFED FLOUNDER
## *with* CRABMEAT STUFFING

1¼ lb. yellowtail sole, boneless and skinless (approximately 8 small filets)
1   lb. Crabmeat Stuffing
3   Tbs. olive oil
1   tsp. sweet paprika
1   lemon, cut into 4 wedges
    Salt and pepper to taste

Set oven on to broil.

Season the sole with salt and pepper and lay on a parchment paper skin side up. Add the crabmeat stuffing on each sole and role the filet.

Brush a 9x12 inch baking sheet pan with oil and arrange the stuffed flounder on the pan. Brush the flounder with oil lightly and sprinkle with paprika. Place the pan in oven about 4–5 inches under broiler and broil for 5–6 minutes or until nicely browned. Transfer the flounder onto 4 plates. Serve with your favorite side dish and lemon wedge.

## CRABMEAT STUFFING

¼   cup unsalted butter
½   cup shallots, finely chopped—you may substitute onion
1   cup white cream sauce (store bought)
⅔   cup Panko bread crumbs
½   lb. lump blue crabmeat
    Salt and pepper to taste

In a sauté pan melt the butter over medium-high heat. Add the shallots and sauté until soft, 4 minutes. Set aside to cool.

Pick through the crabmeat for any shells or cartilage. In a mixing bowl combine the crabmeat and bread crumbs.

In a separate mixing bowl combine the cream sauce and shallot mixture. Fold in the crabmeat and bread crumb mixture to combine. Season with salt and pepper. Keep refrigerated in an air tight container up to 2 days.

## SUSHI RICE

2    cups short grain Japanese sushi rice
½    cup rice vinegar
2    Tbs. Mirin (Japanese sweet sake)
¼    cup sugar

Place the rice in a bowl or rice cooker, insert and add water to cover it generously. Swish the rice in the water in a single direction to rinse off residual starches. Drain the water, refill the bowl or insert, and swish again. Repeat until the water is clear. Do not rub the rice together with your hands because it could break the grains.

Drain the rice, and if not using a rice cooker, place in a medium saucepan fitted with a tight lid. If using a rice cooker, dry the outside of the insert and place it in the cooker. Flatten the rice with the palm of your hand, and without moving your hand, add water until it just touches the highest knuckle of your hand (approximately 2⅓ cups). If using a rice cooker, turn it on and allow the rice to cook. In a saucepan, cover and bring the water to a boil over high heat. Reduce the heat to medium and simmer for 30 minutes. Turn off the heat and let the rice stand, covered, to plump for 20 minutes.

In a small nonreactive saucepan, combine the vinegar, Mirin, and sugar and heat over medium heat until hot, about 2–3 minutes; do not allow the mixture to boil. Keep hot.

Invert the rice into a large bowl. Don't include any browned rice that may have formed in the bottom of the pan. Using a rubber spatula, gently fold the vinegar mixture into the rice. Use a slight, lifting motion to avoid mashing the rice. Taste; the rice should have a pleasingly sweet-acidic edge. If necessary, fold in more of the vinegar mixture.

Dampen a clean dish towel. Gently push the rice together to form a loose mound. Cover with the towel and allow the rice to rest for 20 minutes to develop its flavor. The rice is now ready to use.

Real Seafood Co., Toledo

Gratzi, Charleston

If it's **Italian** flavors you seek —

rustic dishes, authentic urban cuisine or Italian-American

favorites — you'll find that our recipes, like our restau-

rants, are a reflection of Italy's finest regional dining.

We sought out the best flavors of Italy, from the spicy

red sauces of the south, to the aromatic grilled dishes of

Tuscany, to bring you a variety of authentic Italian meals.

We've adapted and refined recipes from multiple regions

to create a distinct cuisine for each restaurant. And, while our menu selections and ambiance vary at each location, fresh, homemade dishes are a constant throughout. We make tantalizingly delicious sauces from scratch every day, using only the freshest spices, herbs and produce. Their quality is assured by the chefs and managers who make sure only the very best ingredients come into our kitchens and are served at our tables. Pasta, sauces, salad dressings — even the coffee — is flavorful, full-bodied and made to order.

Our Italian eateries can seem to be a world apart — even when they're right across the street from one another. We're often asked why we put two restaurants in Ann Arbor, Michigan, Gratzi and Palio, in such close proximity. The answer is simple: each has a distinct menu and atmosphere, different enough to serve a multitude of tastes and occasions. At Gratzi, you can impress a client with upscale, urban, Northern Italian cuisine, in a formal setting — order the Filetto di Manzo, an herb-crusted beef tenderloin served on a portabello mushroom with tomato, goat cheese, roasted potatoes and shallots. At Palio Ristorante, you can treat your family to rustic Italian dishes or traditional Italian-American fare in a fun, down-to-earth, relaxing environment — try the hearty Lasagna, a crowd-pleaser made with ground Italian sausage, fresh spinach, grilled zucchini, mushrooms and Italian cheeses.

Ciao! Ristorante, in Sylvania, Ohio, takes the neighborhood quality of Palio a step further. It features classic Italian cuisine — fresh, homemade dishes that are fragrant, informal and full of character. Zia's, on the waterfront in Toledo, Ohio, offers a taste of country Italian cuisine in a relaxing family-style setting. Perfect for large gatherings, Zia's serves extra-large, Roman-style pizzas — there's

Zia's, Toledo

Ciao!, Toledo

even a pizza delivery service for boats that pull up to the Docks on the Maumee River. For parties of eight or more, try the "Festa di Vitto," which means "celebration of life," and enjoy large platters full of Shrimp, Veal or Chicken Marsala, or Spaghetti Bolognese. Seated around the interior courtyard fountain or gazing up at the forest of Chianti bottles hanging from the ceiling, your dining experience is sure to be a pleasant one.

We've made it a point to give our restaurants, and their menus, a distinct character all their own — and that applies even when they carry the same name. Our newest Gratzi, in Charleston, West Virginia is modeled after piazzas in Florence and Rome and bears absolutely no resemblance to Gratzi in Ann Arbor, which is housed in a restored historical theatre. The Charleston location has a large fireplace in the center, surrounded by cozy, dimly lit rooms, with names such as "The Stone Shed" or "The Blue Room." The menu is unique too. Appetizers such as Ravioli con Salsa di Noci, combine butternut squash and walnut ravioli with creamy sherry and Swiss chard. Entrees include Salmone al Ferri con Mezzaluna — grilled North Atlantic salmon served over Mezzaluna pasta with sautéed spinach and tomatoes in garlic cream sauce.

Whether you choose rustic, urban, Northern or Southern cuisine in a formal or casual atmosphere, authentic Italian meals are a true celebration of life. We encourage you to use the recipes in this section to celebrate your life to the fullest.

Zia's, Toledo

Gratzi, Charleston

Gratzi, Ann Arbor

## ASIAGO AL FORNO
## (BAKED ASIAGO CHEESE)

This dish has become a signature dish of ours. It combines the rustic flavor of Asiago
cheese, thyme and pepper. It is simple to prepare and excellent for an appetizer.

⅓   lb. mild Asiago cheese, cut into ½-inch cubes
½   tsp. fresh thyme leaves, chopped
½   tsp. very coarsely ground fresh pepper
8   slices Italian baguette, sliced into ½-inch thick slices, bias cut

Preheat the oven to 450 degrees. Lay the sliced bread on a baking sheet and place in
oven for 4–5 minutes or until lightly toasted. Remove from oven and set aside.

In a large (2 cups) ceramic dish/casserole add the cubed cheese and bake in oven for
5–6 minutes or until cheese begins to melt. Remove from the oven and place the
casserole dish on a large plate. Sprinkle with fresh thyme and coarsely ground black
pepper. Serve with the toasted bread.

# CARPACCIO *of* BEEF TENDERLOIN
## *with* DIJON MUSTARD AIOLI          Serves 6–8

Carpaccio was invented at Harry's bar in Venice in 1950. It was named for Vittore Carpaccio, the Venetian Renaissance painter whose work was on display in the city that year at a major exhibition. I can think of nothing better than sipping Bellinis and eating carpaccio and saffron risotto at Harry's bar. Carpaccio has been duplicated all over the world, and this is our version.

1½ lb. beef tenderloin, trimmed of fat
1    cup Dijon Aioli
2    cups arugula, stemmed washed and dried
1    cup shiitake mushrooms, stemmed and thinly sliced
¼    cup grated Parmesan, pecorino or other hard cheese
     Freshly ground black pepper to taste

Place the tenderloin in the freezer for at least 20 minutes, to facilitate slicing; ice crystals should form, but the meat should remain pliable.

Remove the tenderloin from the freezer and cut into paper thin slices across the grain with a razor-sharp knife or a meat slicer. Place the slices symmetrically on serving plates so that the whole plate is covered.

In the center of each plate, add arugula and shiitake mushrooms as garnish.

Thin the aioli by whisking in a little milk, chicken stock or water, until it reaches a drizzling consistency. Drizzle over the beef slices, and sprinkle with cheese and freshly ground pepper.

## DIJON AIOLI          Makes 1½ Cups

⅔    cup Dijon mustard
½    cup mayonnaise
2    Tbs. red wine vinegar
1    tsp. fresh lemon juice
1½ tsp. Worcestershire sauce
⅛    tsp. Tabasco sauce
     Salt and pepper to taste

In a small mixing bowl combine all ingredients and mix well.

Keep refrigerated up to one week.

# FRESH PASTA

Pulse in food processor
2½ cups all-purpose flour
½   cup cake flour

Beat together and add to flour
5   eggs
1   Tbs. extra virgin olive oil

Yes, there are hundreds of good dried pasta out there that you can buy, but you want to
make your own for two simple reasons: First, the delicate texture and flour of homemade
is impossible to duplicate in commercially produced pasta. And second, just entertainment
value is worth the effort. The ingredients are simple, but when the pasta starts to flow
from your machine, it practically commands applause. Making pasta is an easy process
to master, but on the other hand it's almost magical.

Talk about simple—this dough consists of just three ingredients: flour, eggs and olive oil.
You've probably heard of pasta made from semolina, a flour made from durum wheat.
It makes a tough dough suited from holding up to the rigors of commercial pasta
machines. But for this pasta, you want a dough that's made from softer flour.

Italians use a fine textured soft flour called "type OO." Italian groceries carry this,
but it's simple to make yourself by using all purpose flour mixed with soft cake flour—
about 5–1 blend.

## Mixing

Using your food processor, it only takes about two minutes, and cleanup is a snap!

First blend the flours in a processor, then with the machine running add all the wet
ingredients gradually. When the dough begins to form a ball, it's ready. But don't
blend it too much, the dough is heavy and could strain your processor's motor.

Next knead a little more flour into the dough by hand so it's not too sticky. Now, divide
the ball of dough into four pieces.

Wrap each piece to keep pasta moist, and let rest for 15 minutes, so it's easier to work with.

## Kneading

Kneading develops a smooth, strong pasta. Since this dough doesn't have the naturally high
amount of gluten that semolina flour provides it's important to knead it well to make it
elastic, soft and pliable. This process is especially easy when you use a pasta machine.
The first part is kneading until you produce a rough-textured dough, fold dough into third
and pass the unfolded edge through rollers 6–8 times until the dough is smooth as velvet.
If the dough starts to tear, sprinkle it with flour then brush off any excess. Tearing means
the dough is too wet and is sticking to the rollers.

Rolling

Once you've finished kneading all the dough it's time to make the pasta—the magical part.

Set the machine on #8 and roll the pasta through, keep rolling and adjusting rollers to next smaller width. Make setting around #4 or #5, cut pasta strips in half so it's easier to handle.

With the dough rolled out, you can easily cut it to make sheets for cannelloni, lasagna or manicotti, or you can roll and cut into strips for pappardelle, linguine or fettuccine. No matter what, after rolling each strip of pasta, cut and store the sheet right away before they dry out.

Palio, Ann Arbor

# CANNELLONI

Cannelloni is one of those delightful mysteries in food. It has a huge flavor and can be quite filling, but at the same time, it's extremely light, chewing is almost optional. Like a good wine, you can swirl it around in your mouth before it melts down your throat.

So what makes cannelloni so different from any other pasta dishes? First it's made with Italian meats like prosciutto and mortadella for flavor impact. Second, both the pasta and filling are intended to be very thin. When it's rolled up, it's on many layers, like puff pastry and croissant; multiple thin layers produce a very tender dish.

Finally, cannelloni is baked in béchamel, a white sauce made with milk, butter and flour. Fresh pasta, a flavorful filling, and simple cream sauce. What's not to love!

To make cannelloni there are a few simple rules, the first being that both pasta and filling have to be thin. The second rule is that the filling is spread over the entire sheet of cooked pasta, not spooned in a thick line across the middle. Finally, the pasta must be rolled like a carpet for a delicate texture.

For the best cannelloni, think thin. First, roll out the pasta as thin as possible–the thinner it is, the softer it will feel in your mouth. Then, to make the most of that delicate texture, spread the filling very thin. A big mouthful of meat isn't the goal, rather just flakes of flavor.

## SPINACH *and*
## THREE CHEESE CANNELLONI
Makes 3 Cups

| | | | | |
|---|---|---|---|---|
| 2 | Tbs. olive oil | | 1 | cup mozzarella, shredded |
| ½ | cup onion, chopped | | ⅔ | cup ricotta cheese |
| 1 | Tbs. garlic, minced | | ½ | cup Parmesan cheese, grated and ½ cup to top of cannelloni |
| 1 | 10 oz. pkg. frozen spinach, defrosted and drained | | 1 | egg, lightly beaten |

Tomato Basil Sauce (see pg. 102)
Béchamel Sauce (see pg. 76)
Salt and pepper to taste

Sauté the onions and garlic in olive oil until softened. Add frozen spinach and cook over low heat until water is evaporated. Set aside to cool. Stir in cheeses, egg, salt and pepper. Fill according to Classic Cannelloni recipe (see pg. 76). Cover with sauce, top with Parmesan cheese and bake in oven.

## CLASSIC CANNELLONI

Sauté in 2 Tbs. unsalted butter and 1 Tbs. vegetable oil:
1    lb. ground meat (veal, chicken, turkey or beef)

Add to sauté
½    cup yellow onion, chopped
1    Tbs. garlic, minced

Deglaze with
¼    cup dry sherry

Process meat mixture with

2    eggs
1    cup Parmesan cheese, grated
¼    lb. prosciutto, diced

¼    lb. mortadella, diced
¼    cup chopped parsley

Tomato Basil Sauce (see pg. 102)
Béchamel Sauce (see below)

Preheat oven to 450 degrees.

Cut the strips of pasta in sheets about 4 inches wide. They can be 5 inches tall. Cook the pasta in plenty of boiling water and cook it about two minutes, until tender but still chewy. Dip them in ice cold water to stop the cooking, then pat them dry—the filling will spread better.

Sauté ground meat in butter and oil in a sauté pan over medium high heat until browned. Add onion, cook until softened. Add minced garlic sautéing only until you smell it. Deglaze pan with sherry, cook until evaporated. Process meat mixture and remaining ingredients in food processor. Pulse until it resembles coarse sawdust. Do not over process.

Before rolling, coat your work surface with parmesan cheese so that cooked pasta does not stick to it. Layout pasta sheets, spread each with 2 Tbs. filling. Gently roll pasta. Keep the seam side down so they don't unravel. Place cannelloni in a lightly sauced (with tomato basil sauce) baking dish. Spoon béchamel on top. Sprinkle with parmesan cheese and bake uncovered for about 20–25 minutes or until parmesan starts to turn golden and sauce bubbles.

## SIMPLE BÉCHAMEL SAUCE

This cream sauce is actually pretty light in consistency. I didn't want anything heavy to cover up the delicate flavors of cannelloni.

5    Tbs. unsalted butter
⅓    cup all-purpose flour
3½ cups milk (whole or 2%)

½    tsp. kosher salt
⅛    tsp. white pepper
⅛    tsp. freshly grated nutmeg (optional)

Melt butter over medium to low heat. Whisk in flour to make roux. Cook and stir two minutes. Gradually add milk to roux. Stir constantly to prevent sticking and cook until thick, about 10 minutes. When thick, add seasoning.

Ciao!, Toledo

Gratzi, Charleston

## CROSTINI AI FUNGHI (TOASTED ITALIAN BAGUETTE *with* WILD MUSHROOMS)

In Toscana, it is called fettunta, "oily slice." In Roma, it is called bruschetta. In many places all over Italy, it is called crostini. It might not even have a definite name, but one thing is for sure, there is nothing better and more basic than a slice of good crusty bread grilled or toasted under the broiler, rubbed lightly with garlic and drizzled with extra virgin olive oil. Today this simple preparation has been updated and the bread is topped by a variety of ingredients.

In their simplest form, they can be used for croutons for soups, as an appetizer, or as an accompaniment to grilled chicken, lamb, beef, or veal; or even cut into small cubes and used as salad croutons. Variations of crostini are endless. We encourage you to try ours and then experiment.

| | | | |
|---|---|---|---|
| 8 | slices Italian baguette, sliced ¾ inch thick | 2 | oz. dried porcini mushrooms |
| ⅓ | cup olive oil | ⅓ | cup dry sherry wine |
| 2 | Tbs. shallots, finely chopped | 1 | cup heavy whipping cream |
| 1 | Tbs. garlic, minced | ⅓ | cup porcini broth |
| ½ | lb. shiitake mushrooms, stemmed, sliced | 2 | tsp. fresh thyme, chopped |
| ½ | lb. cremini mushrooms, sliced | 3 | Tbs. Herb Butter (see pg. 136) |
| | | 3 | Tbs. fresh Italian flat parsley, chopped |
| | | | Coarse salt and ground pepper to taste |

Preheat oven to 450 degrees.

Soak the dry porcini mushrooms in 2 cups of warm water for 15–20 minutes. Drain the mushrooms. Set aside and reserve the broth.

Place the sliced baguette bread on baking sheet pan and toast them in oven for 4–5 minutes or until lightly browned. Remove from oven. Set aside.

In a large sauce pan heat the olive oil over high heat. Add the shallots and garlic and sauté until translucent, 1 minute. Add the mushrooms and continue to sauté over high heat stirring occasionally until they are soft. Deglaze with sherry wine and let it bubble away. Add the heavy cream, porcini broth and thyme. Bring to boil and reduce the liquid to a thick consistency. Stir in herb butter, parsley, salt and pepper. Remove from heat.

Divide the toasted bread among 4 plates. Spoon the mushrooms, including the sauce over the bread.

**Variation:** Substitute chanterelles or morel mushrooms for the shiitake or cremini, or make any combination of these that you like.

# CROSTINI *with* SUN-DRIED TOMATO, ARTICHOKE, *and* OLIVE TAPENADE

Serves 6

18  slices crusty Italian baguette bread, cut ½ inch thick
¼   lb. chunk of Parmesan cheese (for topping crostini)
1   Olive Tapenade
1   Artichoke Tapenade
1   Sun-dried Tomato Tapenade

### Olive Tapenade

1½  cups calamata olives, pitted
½   cup green olives, pitted
3   medium garlic cloves
4   Tbs. capers, rinsed and drained
1   anchovy (optional)

⅓   cup extra virgin olive oil
1   Tbs. Italian flat leaf parsley, chopped
1   tsp. brandy
    Pinch cayenne pepper
    Freshly ground pepper to taste

In a food processor, add the black and green olives, capers, garlic, anchovy and virgin olive oil. Pulse for 20 seconds or until coarsely chopped. Turn the contents into a mixing bowl. Add in the black and cayenne pepper, parsley and brandy and stir well. Set aside.

### Artichoke Tapenade

1   16 oz. can artichoke hearts, well drained
4   Tbs. pine nuts
3   garlic cloves

2   tsp. fresh lemon juice
⅓   cup Parmesan cheese, grated
2   Tbs. flat leaf parsley, chopped
¼   cup extra virgin olive oil
    Coarse salt and ground pepper to taste

Drain the artichokes in a colander and press with your hand to extract more juices. In a food processor, add all the ingredients and process coarsely. Set aside.

### Sun-dried Tomato Tapenade

1   lb. glass jar sun-dried tomatoes, drain the oil
3   medium garlic cloves
½   cup Parmesan cheese
2   Tbs. extra virgin olive oil
    Salt and pepper to taste
    Cayenne pepper to taste

In a food processor add all the ingredients and process coarsely. Set aside.

Preheat the oven to 450 degrees. Place the bread slices on a baking sheet and bake until lightly golden on both sides, about 5 minutes. Remove the bread from the oven. Top the crostini with some of each, the olive, artichoke and sun-dried tomato tapenade. Using a potato peeler, shave the Parmesan cheese and sprinkle over the crostinis. Arrange on individual platters.

## FILETO DI MANZO
(BEEF TENDERLOIN *with* GOAT CHEESE
*and* PORTOBELLO MUSHROOM)

| | | | |
|---|---|---|---|
| 4 | 6 oz. beef tenderloin, center cut, well trimmed | 1 | cup Cabernet Sauvignon Sauce (see pg. 118) |
| 4 | small portobello mushrooms, stems removed | 1½ | Tbs. fresh thyme, chopped |
| 4 | goat cheese slices, sliced ¼ inch thick | ¼ | cup milk |
| 1 | large tomato, sliced ¼ inch thick | ¼ | cup flour |
| 16 | shallots, peeled | 1 | cup olive oil |
| ½ | lb. Yukon gold potatoes | 1 | Tbs. balsamic vinegar |
| ½ | lb. asparagus, ends trimmed, blanched | 1 | clove garlic, minced |
| | | 1 | leek, cut into fine strips, washed and drained |
| | | | Coarse salt and ground black pepper |

Preheat oven to 400 degrees. Prepare gas or charcoal grill.

In a large mixing bowl combine balsamic vinegar, 2 Tbs. olive oil, garlic, ½ Tbs. thyme, salt and pepper. Mix well. Toss in the portobello mushroom to combine. Set aside.

In a large mixing bowl add the potatoes, 1 Tbs. thyme, 2 Tbs. oil, salt and pepper. Toss to coat. Place the potatoes on a parchment paper lined baking sheet and bake in oven for 20 minutes or until browned and tender. Set aside keeping warm.

In a small mixing bowl toss the shallots, with 1 Tbs. oil, salt and pepper. Place in a small roasting pan and cover with aluminum foil and bake for 15–20 minutes or until nicely browned and tender. Set aside keeping warm.

Dip the leeks into the milk. In a small frying pan heat the ½ cup of oil to 350 degrees. Remove the leeks from milk and coat with flour and fry in hot oil for 2 minutes or until crispy. Remove and place on paper towel. Set aside.

Rub the filets with oil and season with salt and pepper and grill on a hot grill for 5–6 minutes on each side for medium rare or longer for more doneness. Keep warm. Meanwhile, toss the asparagus with light oil and salt and pepper, and grill asparagus for 2–3 minutes on both sides or until the asparagus is hot. Set aside keeping warm.

Grill the portobello mushrooms on both sides for 4–5 minutes or until tender. Also grill the tomatoes on both sides briefly. Heat the Cabernet Sauvignon Sauce until hot.

### Assembly

In the center of each warmed individual plate, place the portobello mushroom. Top with a slice of tomato, goat cheese, and beef tenderloin. Spoon the sauce around fillets. Arrange the shallots, potatoes and asparagus around fillets and top each fillet with a crispy leek.

# FOUR CHEESE LASAGNA *with* ITALIAN SAUSAGE, MUSHROOM *and* ZUCCHINI

This is the familiar hearty Southern Neapolitan-style lasagna, bulging with sausage, mushrooms and cheeses. This is our version.

### For the mixture

| | |
|---|---|
| 1½ lb. mild Italian sausage, coarsely ground | 1   lb. zucchini, sliced lengthwise into ¼ inch thick slices |
| 2   Tbs. unsalted butter | 2   cups fresh spinach, coarsely chopped |
| 1   leek, white only, finely chopped, washed and drained | 1   tsp. fresh oregano |
| | 1   Tbs. fresh basil |
| 1   small fennel bulb, finely chopped | 1   Tbs. flour |
| 1½ cups mushrooms, sliced | 1   cup heavy cream |
| | Coarse salt to taste |
| | Ground black pepper to taste |

### For lasagne

| | |
|---|---|
| 2   eggs | 1   cup Parmesan cheese |
| 15  lasagna noodles (about 12 ounces) | 4   cups mozzarella cheese, grated |
| 2   15 oz. containers part-skim ricotta cheese | 1½ cups fontina cheese, grated |
| | 4   cups Tomato Basil Sauce (see pg. 102) |

### Making the mixture

Preheat the oven to 350 degrees.

In a sauce pan add the Italian sausage with ¼ cup of water and cook over medium-high heat, stirring often to break up the meat. Cook until sausage is no longer pink. Drain the sausage and set aside.

Melt the butter in a large sauce pan. Add the chopped leek and fennel and sauté over medium heat for 8–10 minutes or until tender. Add the mushrooms and continue to sauté until they are soft. Stir in flour, then add heavy cream, basil, oregano, salt and pepper. Bring to boil and cook for 2–3 minutes, stirring occasionally. Stir in the chopped spinach and cook for 2 minutes or until wilted. Remove from heat. Mix in the drained Italian sausage. Set aside.

Arrange the sliced zucchini on a parchment paper lined baking sheet and season with salt and pepper. Bake in the oven for 10 minutes. Remove from the oven and set aside.

### Making the lasagna

Cook noodles in a large pot of salted boiling water until almost tender but still firm to bite, about 7 minutes. Drain and cover with cold water.

In a large bowl, beat the eggs and mix in ricotta. Season with salt and pepper.

In a separate bowl, combine remaining cheeses.

Drain pasta and pat dry. Grease sides and bottom of a 13x9 inch glass baking dish. Spread ½ cup tomato sauce over bottom of baking pan. Place 5 noodles over sauce, overlapping a bit. Spread half of ricotta mixture evenly over noodles, then spread sausage mixture as well. Sprinkle ⅓ of cheeses evenly over sausage and ricotta mixture. Repeat layering with

5 noodles, remaining ricotta, sausage mixture and ½ the amount of remaining cheeses. Arrange remaining 5 noodles to cover it all. Sprinkle remaining cheeses evenly over lasagna. (Can be prepared up to 1 day ahead. If doing so, at this point, cover tightly with plastic wrap and refrigerate until next day.) Cover baking dish with aluminum foil. Bake lasagna 30 minutes; uncover and continue baking until hot and golden on top, about 20 minutes. Let lasagna stand 15 minutes before serving.

Meanwhile, heat the tomato sauce, spoon some sauce on the plates and top with lasagna.

## INSALATA CAPRESE                                        Serves 4

2    3 oz. balls of fresh mozzarella, cut into ¼ inch thick slices
1    each of red, orange, and yellow heirloom tomatoes, cut into ¼ inch slices
8    large fresh basil leaves
4    Tbs. Balsamic Syrup
4    Tbs. Basil Oil
     Coarse salt and freshly ground pepper to taste

In the center of individual plates, place orange tomato slices. Top with mozzarella cheese.
    Then top with red tomato slices, then again mozzarella cheese, and finally top with slices
    of yellow tomato. Put one basil leaf on top of each yellow tomato. Cut the remaining basil
    leaves into chiffonades.

Spoon the Balsamic Syrup and Basil Oil around tomato and mozzarella towers and sprinkle
    with basil chiffonades. Season with salt and pepper.


## BALSAMIC SYRUP                                        Makes 1 Cup

This syrup is wonderful for salads and over fresh berries, as well as many other dishes.

2    cups well-aged balsamic vinegar

Place the vinegar in a saucepan. Bring to a boil and lower the heat to simmer. Reduce to
    about 1 cup. Remove from heat and cool. Store in an airtight container or squeezable
    bottle at room temperature.


## BASIL OIL                                        Makes 1½ Cups

This fragrant oil adds herby flavor to crab and lobster cake, basil mashed potatoes and
    other grilled dishes, or for superior vinaigrettes and aiolis.

Store it in an airtight container, where it will last for about 1 week. It will darken in time,
    but the flavor remains excellent. Shake it before using.

2    cups basil leaves
1    cup spinach leaves
1    cup olive oil
½    tsp. salt

In a large sauce pan, bring salted water to a boil (about 1 gallon).

Plunge in the basil and spinach and cook until soft, but still green, about 1 minute.
    Drain and transfer the greens to ice cold water to chill. When cold, remove and
    squeeze excess water from the greens. Pat them dry in a clean towel.

Transfer the vegetables to a blender. Add the oil and salt and blend until smooth, about
    3 minutes. Remove the oil and use, or store.

## ITALIAN COBB SALAD

The original Cobb Salad was created in 1936 at Hollywood's famous Brown Derby Restaurant by Robert Cobb, who was then the proprietor. This version is given a distinctive Italian flair by the addition of Pancetta, Cambazola cheese and roasted garlic. Cambazola is a creamy blue cheese from Italy, and any similar cheese can be substituted.

| | |
|---|---|
| ¼ cup olive oil | 1 bunch arugula, rinsed and dried |
| 1 tsp. fresh sage, chopped | 1 head Belgian endive, rinsed and dried |
| 1 tsp. fresh thyme, picked | 1 small head green romaine, |
| 1 tsp. fresh rosemary, chopped | rinsed and dried |
| 1 lb. chicken breast, | ½ cup basil leaves |
| boneless and skinless | 4 eggs, hard cooked and chopped |
| Salt and freshly ground | 3 large, ripe Roma tomatoes, diced, |
| black pepper to taste | 4 oz. Cambazola cheese, or similar |
| 1½ cups Roasted Garlic Dressing (see pg. 144) | flavored cheese, crumbled |
| 8 thinly sliced pancetta, diced | 4 scallions, finely chopped |
| 1 small head raddichio, rinsed and dried | (green and white part) |

In a mixing bowl add olive oil, sage, thyme, rosemary, salt and pepper and mix. Add in the chicken breast to combine and marinate for 3–4 hours. Keep refrigerated.

Grill the chicken breast for 5–6 minutes on each side until done and cut into ½ inch dice, and set aside.

Sauté the pancetta until crisp and the fat is rendered. Drain on paper towels and set aside.

Slice the radicchio into large shreds and chop crosswise. Remove the stems from the arugula and separate the endive leaves. De-rib the head of romaine and then tear into bite size pieces. Place the greens and basil in a large bowl and toss gently to combine. Transfer the mixed greens to a large platter. In circles, rows, or decorative patterns, place the chicken, eggs, tomatoes, cheese, pancetta and scallions over the greens.

Bring the salad platter to the table, pour the dressing over the salad, and toss well.
Serve with a basket of crusty Italian bread (optional).

## LINGUINE DEL GOLFO

Serves 4

¼  cup olive oil
8   jumbo shrimp, peeled and
½   lb. natural sea scallops
½   red bell pepper, cut into fine strips
1   cup dry white wine

1½  cups Chicken Stock (see pg. 147)
1   cup Basil Pesto Sauce (see below)
2   dz. mussels, well scrubbed
1   lb. dried linguine
Coarse salt to taste
Freshly ground pepper to taste

In a large skillet or saucepan, heat the olive over medium high heat. Add the scallops, shrimp and red pepper strips and sauté for one minute, turning shrimp and scallops over.

Deglaze with ½ cup of white wine, add the chicken broth, bring to boil and cook the seafood for 1 minute.

Meanwhile, cook the linguine in a large pot of salted water over high heat until al dente, 8–10 minutes. Drain and toss the pasta with shrimp, scallops. Stir in the pesto sauce. Season with salt and pepper if necessary.

Meanwhile, cook the mussels in a large pot over high heat with remaining wine and ½ cup of water. Cover and cook until all the mussels open, about 4 minutes. Discard any mussels that don't open.

Transfer the pasta with tongs evenly into four bowls and surround with mussels.

## PESTO BASILICO (BASIL, PARMESAN *and* PINE NUT SAUCE)

Makes 1½ Cups

There are few sauces that compare with this renowned creation from Genoa. Originally, and in some places still, pesto is made with a mortar and pestle; hence, the word "pesto" which derives from the verb "pestare," meaning "to pound." Use the most fragrant basil and the best olive oil and parmesan available. Serve pesto over pasta, pizza, or a salad, or use it as a dipping sauce or as an enhancement for vegetable soup.

2   cups fresh basil leaves,
     loosely packed
2   medium size garlic cloves
½   cup fresh grated Parmesan cheese,
     preferably Parmigiano-Reggiano

1   cup extra virgin olive oil
½   cup pine nuts
1½  tsp. coarse salt or to taste
1   tsp. ground black pepper or to taste

In a food processor or blender, combine basil, garlic, pine nuts, salt and pepper, and blend until thoroughly combined. Add grated cheese and olive oil, and blend to a smooth consistency.

If pesto sauce is not used right away, store in an airtight container, refrigerate for up to 4 days, or keep frozen for up to 2–3 months.

## OSSO BUCCO DI AGNELLO
## (BRAISED LAMB SHANK)

Serves 4

| | | | | |
|---|---|---|---|---|
| 4 | lamb shanks (approximately 1 lb. each shank) | | 1 | qt. Chicken Stock (see pg. 147) |
| 3 | oz. olive oil | | 1 | qt. chopped tomato, canned |
| 1 | medium onion, ¼-inch diced | | 2 | Tbs. fresh basil, coarsely chopped |
| 3 | stalks celery, ¼-inch diced | | 2 | Tbs. fresh thyme, chopped |
| 2 | medium carrots, ¼-inch diced | | ½ | cup Veal Demi Glace (see pg. 146) |
| ½ | cup flour | | 2 | Tbs. chopped parsley |
| 2 | cups dry white wine | | | Coarse salt to taste |
| | | | | Freshly ground pepper to taste |

In a large sauté pan, heat olive oil over high heat. Season lamb shanks with salt and pepper and dust in flour. Shake excess off. Add the lamb shanks to sauté pan and sear all sides until nicely browned.

Transfer the shanks into a roasting pan—4 inches deep (Dutch oven). Add onions, celery, carrots and garlic to sauté pan and sauté the vegetables until translucent, stirring occasionally.

Deglaze the pan with white wine and reduce to half. Pour in the Chicken Stock and chopped tomatoes. Add fresh basil, thyme, salt and pepper. Bring to a boil. Pour the sauce over lamb shank. Cover (seal) with foil and cook in oven at 350 degrees for 2 hours. Remove from oven. Transfer the lamb shanks to a holding pan (covered). Place the pan with sauce over high heat. Whisk in the Veal Demi Glace until incorporated.

Transfer the lamb shanks to individual plates or a platter. Then spoon the sauce over all and sprinkle with chopped parsley. We recommend serving this dish with mashed potatoes.

## MINESTRONE ALLA GENOVESE
## (MINESTRONE GENOA STYLE)

| | |
|---|---|
| 2   Tbs. olive oil | 2   cups spinach, washed, drained, coarsely chopped |
| 2   Tbs. unsalted butter | ½   cup dried white beans |
| ½   cup onion, finely chopped | 2½ qts. chicken stock (see pg. 147) |
| 1   leek, white part only, finely sliced, washed and drained | 1   large tomato, blanched, peeled, seeded, diced, or ⅔ cup canned diced tomato, drained |
| 1   cup carrots, peeled, cut into ½-inch dice | 2   Tbs. chicken base |
| ½   small head Savoy cabbage, trimmed, cut into 1-inch cubes | Salt and pepper to taste |
| 1   cup potatoes, peeled, cut into ½-inch dice | ½   cup Pesto Basilico (see pg. 90) |
| | ½   cup elbow macaroni |
| | Parmesan cheese, shredded (optional) |

Soak the beans overnight in water. Refrigerate. Drain and rinse the beans, and add to a small saucepan. Cover with water. Bring to a boil and simmer for 30–35 minutes or until tender. Set aside.

In a large heavy bottomed soup pot, heat the oil and butter over medium heat. Add the onion, leek, carrots and Savoy cabbage and toss to coat with oil and butter. Sauté for 10 minutes stirring occasionally.

Add the Chicken Stock and chicken base, and bring to a boil. Then add the potatoes and diced tomatoes. When it comes to a boil, turn the heat down to simmer for 8–10 minutes or until potatoes are tender. Drain the beans and add to the soup along with the spinach.

Meanwhile, cook the elbow macaroni in boiling salted water for 8–10 minutes or until al dente. Drain the pasta and add to the soup. Check the seasoning.

Ladle the soup into individual bowls, dollop with Pesto Basilico and sprinkle on some Parmesan cheese.

# RIGATONI COUNTRY STYLE

1   lb. coarsely ground mild Italian sausage
⅔   cup dry cannelini beans
½   cup olive oil
½   cup onion, finely diced
½   cup celery, finely diced
4   Tbs. garlic, minced
3   cups Chicken Stock (see pg. 147)
2   cups escarole, washed, drained
     and cut into bite size pieces

1   cup fresh tomatoes, diced and seeded
1   Tbs. fresh oregano, chopped
1   lb. dried rigatoni
     Salt and pepper to taste
     Dried red pepper flakes, optional
     Parmesan or Romano cheese,
        grated, optional

Soak the beans overnight in water. Refrigerate. Rinse the beans, and add to a small
   saucepan. Cover with water. Bring to a boil and simmer for 30–35 minutes or until tender.
   Drain and set aside.

Cook the Italian sausage in a saucepan, covered with water, stirring occasionally, until the
   meat is no longer pink. Drain well and set aside.

In a large saucepan heat the olive oil over medium heat. Add the onion, celery and garlic
   and sauté until translucent, about 5 minutes. Add the Chicken Stock, sausage, escarole,
   beans, tomatoes, oregano, salt, pepper, and pepper flakes. Toss all together well and
   continue to cook over medium high heat until escarole becomes wilted.

Meanwhile, cook the rigatoni in boiling salted water for 8–10 minutes or until al dente
   (firm). Drain the pasta and toss with sausage mixture. Spoon the pasta into each
   individual bowl and sprinkle with grated cheese.

# POLLO AL MARSALA CON FUNGHI
(CHICKEN BREAST *with* PORCINI
MUSHROOMS *and* MARSALA)                    Serves 4

1½ lb. chicken breasts—boned, skinned,
    and halved, rinsed and patted dry
4   Tbs. olive oil
4   Tbs. unsalted butter
½  cup unbleached all-purpose flour,
    evenly spread over a sheet of
    aluminum foil
1   medium size onion,
    finely chopped—about ¾ cup

2   oz. dry porcini mushrooms,
    soaked in 2 cups warm water
    for 15–20 minutes
⅔  cup pancetta, cut into ¼-inch dice
½  cup dry Marsala wine
½  cup Chicken Stock (see pg. 147)
½  cup mushroom broth
    Salt and pepper to taste

Soak the dry porcini mushrooms in 2 cups of warm water for 15–20 minutes. Drain the
mushrooms. Set aside and reserve the broth.

Place the chicken breasts on a flat surface between plastic wrap. Using a meat mallet,
pound to between ¼–½ inches thickness for faster cooking.

Season the chicken breast with salt and pepper. Coat the chicken liberally with flour and
shake off any excess.

Heat the oil in a large skillet over medium heat. Add the pancetta and cook until halfway
rendered. Add the chicken, making sure not to crowd the skillet (the chicken can be
browned in two batches). Cook until it is lightly golden on both sides, 4–5 minutes.

Add the pancetta and cook, stirring occasionally for 2 minutes or until rendered down.
Add the onions and cook stirring occasionally for 2 minutes, or until translucent. Add the
mushrooms and continue to cook stirring occasionally for 30 seconds. Add the wine and
let it bubble away. Add the Chicken Stock and mushroom broth, salt and pepper. Whisk in
the unsalted butter to combine. Transfer the chicken to the serving plates and spoon the
sauce over the chicken.

Note: This dish may be served with mashed potatoes, rice pilaf, or noodles as an
accompaniment.

## SPAGHETTI BOLOGNESE

6  cups Bolognese (Meat) Sauce
1  cup heavy whipping cream
1½ lb. dried spaghetti
2  cups imported Parmesan cheese, shredded
   Coarse salt to taste
   Freshly ground black pepper

In a large saucepan heat the Bolognese Sauce and heavy whipping cream. Season with salt and pepper.

Meanwhile, cook the spaghetti in a large pot of salted water over high heat until al dente, 8–10 minutes. Drain and use tongs to transfer the pasta to individual bowls. Then spoon the Bolognese sauce over all. Serve with plenty of Parmesan cheese.

## SALSA BOLOGNESE (MEAT SAUCE)

1  onion, peeled and minced, about 1 cup
1  carrot, peeled and minced, about 1 cup
½  bulb fennel, minced, about 1 cup
2  cloves garlic, minced
¼  cup extra virgin olive oil
4  Tbs. unsalted butter

1  lb. ground veal
¾  cup prosciutto, chopped (optional)
1  cup white wine, dry
2  lb. ripe tomatoes, blanched, peeled, seeded and chopped
1  Tbs. coarse salt
1½ tsp. ground black pepper
1  tsp. lemon rind (optional)
2  Tbs. fresh sage, coarsely chopped

Finely mince the onion, carrot and fresh fennel. You may do this by hand or in a food processor.

Heat the olive oil and butter in a heavy-bottomed pot over medium heat. Add the minced vegetables, including garlic. Sauté over low heat, stirring occasionally, until they are very soft, 8–10 minutes.

Add the veal and prosciutto, raise the heat and cook, stirring until the meat is no longer pink.

Add the wine and cook gently, stirring occasionally, until almost all the wine has evaporated, about 5 minutes. Add the tomatoes, salt, pepper, fresh sage and lemon rind. Stir well, cover the pan and reduce the heat to medium-low and let simmer 45 minutes, until the sauce has a medium-thick consistency. If the sauce is too thick, add a little meat stock or water.

Note: Instead of using fresh ripe tomatoes, you can substitute two 24 oz. cans of chopped tomatoes. This sauce is wonderful with rigatoni or penne. It is equally delicious with a lighter pasta like pappardelle or fettuccine noodles.

Variation: You may substitute 1 pound ground pork or beef for the veal, or a combination.

At Zia's we add 1 cup heavy cream to the sauce at the end. This makes a creamy, rich texture to the sauce that works particularly well with veal.

## POLLO PARMIGIANA (BREADED CHICKEN BREAST *with* PARMESAN)

Serves 4

| | | | |
|---|---|---|---|
| 1 | egg | 1 | Tbs. fresh basil, chopped |
| ¼ | cup milk | 1 | Tbs. fresh oregano, chopped |
| ¼ | cup flour | ¼ | cup chopped parsley |
| 3 | cups Panko bread crumbs | 4 | 5 oz. skinless, boneless chicken breast |
| 1 | Tbs. minced garlic | | Coarse salt and ground black pepper |
| ½ | cup Parmesan cheese, grated | | |

Cooking and assembling the chicken

- ⅓ cup olive oil
- 2 cups Tomato Basil Sauce (see below)
- ½ lb. spaghetti, cooked al dente
- 4 slices mozzarella cheese, thinly sliced
- 2 Tbs. Parmesan cheese, grated
- 4 fresh basil leaves, as garnish

Heat the oven to 400 degrees.

In a large mixing bowl combine the bread crumbs, garlic, Parmesan, basil, oregano, and parsley, and mix well. Set aside. In a separate bowl beat the egg with the milk. Set aside. In another bowl add the flour and set aside. Season the chicken breast with salt and pepper. Dust the chicken breast lightly in flour, then dip in egg wash. Coat the chicken breast on both sides with breading and press lightly with hand to adhere. Set aside.

Heat the oil in a large sauté pan over medium-high heat. Add the chicken and sauté on each side for approximately 3 minutes or until nicely browned. Remove the chicken from the heat and place on a baking sheet. Top with mozzarella slices and sprinkle with Parmesan cheese. Bake in oven for 2 minutes or until cheese melts.

In a large sauce pan, heat the Tomato Basil Sauce along with spaghetti. Transfer the spaghetti with tongs to individual plates and top each with a chicken breast.

## SUGO DI POMODORE (TOMATO BASIL SAUCE)

Makes 2 Quarts

| | | | |
|---|---|---|---|
| 3 | 24-oz. cans chopped tomatoes, preferably Hunts | 2 | cups fresh basil leaves, loosely packed, coarsely chopped |
| ½ | cup extra virgin olive oil | 1½ | Tbs. coarse salt |
| 6 | medium size garlic cloves | 2 | tsp. freshly ground black pepper |
| ⅓ | cup tomato puree | 1 | Tbs. honey or pinch of sugar (optional) |

In a food processor or blender, puree the olive oil and garlic. Pour the mixture into a medium size sauce pan and heat over medium heat. Be careful not to burn the garlic. Stir in chopped tomatoes, tomato puree, salt and pepper. Bring to boil, stirring occasionally. Reduce the heat to low and simmer for 30 minutes. Stir in honey and fresh basil. Makes about 10 cups.

# RISOTTO ALLA PRIMAVERA
## (RISOTTO *with* SPRING VEGETABLES *and* PARMESAN TUILES)

Serves 4–6

**For the Parmesan tuiles**

| | |
|---|---|
| 1 | cup grated Parmesan cheese |
| 1½ | cup microgreens |

**Spring vegetables**

| | |
|---|---|
| 2 | Tbs. olive oil |
| 2 | Tbs. garlic, minced |
| 1 | lb. assorted wild mushrooms, stemmed and diced small |
| 1 | zucchini, small diced |
| 1 | red pepper, stemmed, seeded, and diced small |
| 1 | yellow pepper, stemmed, seeded and diced small |
| 4 | oz. spinach, stemmed and chopped small |
| 4 | asparagus, ends trimmed, or 12 sugar snap peas, sliced |
| | Coarse salt and freshly ground pepper to taste |

**Risotto**

| | |
|---|---|
| 4 | Tbs. unsalted butter |
| 1 | Tbs. olive oil |
| ⅓ | cup finely chopped shallots |
| 1½ | cup arborio rice |
| 1 | cup dry white wine |
| 6 | cups Chicken Stock (see pg. 147) |
| | Coarse salt and freshly ground pepper to taste |
| ¼ | cup Parmesan cheese, grated |

For the Parmesan tuiles, preheat the oven to 350 degrees and invert 6 small cups onto a flat work surface. Arrange six 4-inch ring molds on a parchment-lined sheet pan and sprinkle the parmesan inside of each to form six rounds. Place in the oven and bake for 3–4 minutes. Remove from the oven, and using a spatula, transfer the tuiles to the inverted cups to cool.

For the vegetables, in a large sauce pan, heat the oil over medium heat; add the garlic and sauté until translucent. Add the mushrooms and sauté until tender. Add the zucchini, red and yellow peppers, asparagus (or sugar snap peas) and spinach, and cook, stirring occasionally until the vegetables are tender, about 4 minutes. Season with salt and pepper and set aside.

For the risotto, in a large sauce pan, bring the stock to a boil over high heat. Reduce the heat to a low simmer. In a large heavy-bottomed sauce pan, heat 2 tablespoons of the butter with the olive oil over medium heat. Add the shallots and cook, stirring often, until they are softened, about 4 minutes.

Reduce the heat to medium low. Add the rice and cook, stirring almost constantly, until the rice is glistening and has turned milky opaque white, 3 minutes. Add the wine, and cook until the liquid has been absorbed by the rice. Add 1 cup of the simmering stock into the rice. Cook, stirring often, until the stock has been almost completely absorbed, about 2 minutes. Add another cup of stock. Continue cooking and stirring, adding more stock only when previous addition has been completely absorbed. After 15 minutes, begin tasting the rice. At this point, add the remaining stock. The rice should be firm, yet cooked through, in about 18 minutes total cooking time. During the last 2 minutes, add the reserved vegetables.

Remove from the heat, stir in the remaining 2 tablespoons of butter and Parmesan cheese to combine. Season and set aside, keeping warm.

To serve, spoon the risotto into 4 large warmed soup bowls. Place a Parmesan tuile on top and fill with microgreens.

# SALTIMBOCCA DI VITELLO ALLA ROMANA
## (VEAL SCALOPPINE *with* PROSCIUTTO)    Serves 4

We have Roman culinary smarts to thank for this wonderful combination of veal, prosciutto, sage, and wine, which characterizes this dish. Saltimbocca is meant to be good enough to "jump into the mouth," as its name implies.

| | |
|---|---|
| 1 lb. veal scalloppine, from the top round, cut into ⅛-inch thick pounded thin (approx. 8 slices) | 4 Tbs. olive oil |
| | ½ cup dry sherry wine |
| 4 Tbs. fresh sage, coarsely chopped or 3 tsp. dried, crumbled | ½ cup unbleached all-purpose flour, evenly spread over a sheet of aluminum foil |
| ¼ lb. thinly sliced prosciutto | ½ cup Veal or Chicken Stock (see pg. 147) |
| 4 Tbs. unsalted butter | Salt and pepper to taste |

Season one side of veal scaloppini with sage and salt and pepper. Top each piece of veal with a slice of prosciutto and press lightly with your fingers. Coat the veal liberally with the flour and shake off excess.

Heat the oil in a large skillet over medium-high heat. Add the veal slices with prosciutto side down first, making sure not to crowd the skillet. Sauté the veal in batches until lightly golden brown on both sides, about 1 minute. Turn the veal and cook for 1 minute more.

Arrange the veal on serving plates. Add the sherry wine to the skillet and reduce it by half over medium-high heat, scrapping up the brown bits that cling to the pan. Pour in the veal stock and reduce a bit more. Whisk in unsalted butter and remainder of sage. Season with salt and pepper and pour the sauce over the veal.

## ZUPPA DI VONGOLE E COZZE
### (STEAMED CLAMS *and* MUSSELS *with* ZUCCHINI *and* PEPPERS)

Serves 4

⅓   cup extra virgin olive oil
⅓   cup chopped fresh flat leaf parsley
4    large garlic cloves, minced
¼    tsp. crushed hot red pepper flakes
2    tsp. fresh thyme, chopped
2    Tbs. canola oil
¼    cup shallots, chopped
1    red bell pepper, seeded,
       cut into fine strips

1    yellow bell pepper, seeded,
       cut into fine strips
1    small zucchini, cut into fine strips
1½   dz. little neck clams, well scrubbed
1½   dz. mussels, well scrubbed
⅔    cup dry white wine
⅔    cup water
4    Tbs. unsalted butter
     Coarse salt to taste

In a small bowl, mix the olive oil, parsley, garlic, thyme and dry red peppers. Set aside.

In a large sauce pan, heat the canola oil over medium-high heat. Add the shallots and sauté until translucent, 3 minutes. Add the zucchini and peppers and continue to sauté for 2 minutes. Add the clams, wine and water to cover. Cook for 3 minutes, until some of the clams have opened and released their juices. Add the mussels, oil mixture, butter and salt. Cover and cook until all the clams and mussels open, about 4 minutes.

Transfer the clams and mussels to individual bowls using tongs. Then spoon the clam broth over all. Serve with basket of crusty bread to soak up the juices.

# Steaks

and chops that are a cut above the rest: That was our vision for our premier American chop houses, so we provide the exceptional quality of food and service that makes them stand out in each marketplace.

We have three locations for The Chop House — Ann Arbor and Grand Rapids, Michigan; and Charleston, West Virgina. All are distictive, a la carte, steak houses serving USDA prime steaks, premium seafood and time-honored sides. In each restaurant, we use the highest quality of meat — the top two percent of beef in the United States. Entrees like Filet Mignon and New York Strip Steak with Herb Butter are prepared from USDA prime beef, and we use exclusive cuts of meat for non-beef dishes like Australian Rib Lamb Chops and Roasted Rack of Venison.

Service in all three chop houses sets a new standard for our industry. The Ann Arbor location instituted a team approach — two servers per table — and synchronized food delivery so that everyone at each table is served simultaneously. That process has been so successful that it is now being replicated in the other locations, thanks, in part, to the Ann Arbor staff. The Chop House service staff in Ann Arbor took such pride in their restaurant's reputation that, on their own time, they produced a training videotape of their procedures to send to The Chop House employees in Charleston, West Virginia.

Before we opened The Chop House in Ann Arbor, the city was lacking a great, upscale steakhouse. It just made sense to launch the restaurant with a separate-but-connected, equally-upscale dessert salon: La Dolce Vita. This concept has been so well-received, we opened the Grand Rapids location with a La Dolce Vita section, too. Located in the heart of downtown Grand Rapids, directly across from the Amway Grand Plaza, The Chop House is perfect for special nights out or for entertaining business clients.

The Chop House in Charleston, West Virginia, is recognized as one of the city's finest restaurants. Its outstanding menu of steaks and chops, including

The Chop House, Ann Arbor

The Chop House, Charleston

The Chop House, Ann Arbor

Beef Wellington and Roasted Venison Rack, and rich elegance, with a private dining room within the main dining room, make it the place to go when you have an extraordinary event to celebrate.

Although meat is the specialty at the three restaurants, it's the service and the signature dishes — Lobster Bisque and Potatoes Au Gratin — that people can't stop talking about. The secret behind our famous Lobster Bisque? We start from scratch, using a live lobster. It takes a little more time and expense to do it right — and people can taste the difference. As for the Potatoes Au Gratin: We use a good, sharp New York cheddar cheese, with heavy cream and butter, layering 11 or 12 pounds of large Idaho potatoes sliced to a thickness of about ⅛- to ¹⁄₁₆-inch thick. It's a very time-consuming process, but guests are delighted by the result: golden brown wedges served piping hot.

Our chop houses are a destination place for friends and family, and your dinner table can be, too. Just treat your guests to the premier recipes in this section. The service is up to you!

Carson's, Fort Myers

Carson's, Fort Myers

The Chop House, Grand Rapids

# BAKED FRENCH ONION SOUP

The real flavor of classic onion soup comes from the caramelized onions and good brown
veal stock. This is a long process, up to 1½ hours, and cannot be rushed.

| | | | |
|---|---|---|---|
| 1 | stick + 2 Tbs. unsalted butter | 5 | sprigs fresh thyme |
| 4 | lb. onions, peeled and thinly sliced | 1 | French baguette bread, cut into ½ inch thick slices |
| 4 | Tbs. garlic, minced | | |
| 1 | cup dry white wine | 1 | lb. imported Gruyere swiss cheese, shredded |
| ½ | cup dry sherry wine | | |
| 3 | Tbs. flour, all-purpose | ¼ | lb. imported Parmesan cheese, shredded |
| 2 | qts. Brown Beef Stock (see pg. 146) | | Coarse salt and pepper to taste |

### Caramelizing the onions

For good caramelized onions, use a heavy bottomed sauce pan, you don't want hot spots that
could possibly burn the onions.

Melt the butter over medium-high heat.

Place the sliced onions in the covered pan and sweat them until the big pile reduces and
becomes clear. Remove the lid and let the onions cook slightly. Be sure to stir them often.
What is happening is that carbohydrates in the onions are breaking down into sugar as
heat is applied. These sugars then turn a rich brown color (the same reaction when white
sugar is heated, melts and turns into caramel). The deeper brown the onions get the
richer the flavor.

Add chopped garlic and continue cooking for an additional 5 minutes.

Add the wine and sherry. Turn up the heat to reduce wines until evaporated (about
10 minutes).

Add flour and stir. Cook to remove the starch of the flour (about 3–4 minutes).

Stir in Brown Beef Stock. Tie the thyme bundle with butcher string and add to soup with
salt and pepper. Simmer for 30 minutes. Keep warm.

### Topping the soup

Preheat the oven to 400 degrees. On a baking sheet pan place the sliced bread in oven
for 5–6 minutes until dry. Remove from oven. Set aside.

Ladle 10 oz. of soup into individual crocks on baking sheet. Top with slices of dry
French bread.

Combine cheeses. Sprinkle 1 cup over each soup crock. Pile on right up to the edge.
Bake the crocks of soup in 400 degree oven for 10 minutes or until cheese is browned
and bubbly.

## BEEFSTEAK TOMATO
## *and* VIDALIA ONION SALAD

Serves 4–6

Beefsteak tomatoes, with their ribbed sides or lobes, identify the biggest tomato of all. Perfect for fresh eating, one slice can cover a whole sandwich. You'll see varieties like Mortgage lifter, Better Boy, Brandywine, Goliath, and Big Boy. Careful storing is critical to preserving that fresh taste. Tomatoes don't like to be cold—never refrigerate them. Temperatures below 50 degrees damage cell membranes, making them mealy and flavorless. Tomatoes prefer a more temperate storage environment of about 65–70 degrees. The kitchen counter is probably the best place. Store them in a single layer, away from sunlight—direct sun promotes mushiness, not ripening.

4   Beefsteak or heirloom tomatoes, cored, cut into ¼-inch thick slices
2   small Vidalia onions, peeled, cut into ⅛-inch thick slices
3   cups mesclun lettuce
1   cup Roquefort cheese, or any other creamy blue cheese, crumbled
1   cup White Balsamic Vinaigrette (see pg. 144)
¼   cup fresh chives, finely chopped

Place the greens on individual plates. Arrange the tomato and Vidalia onion slices over the mesclun. Drizzle the vinaigrette over the salads and top with crumbled bleu cheese and fresh chives.

## CABERNET SAUCE

Makes 2½ Cups

¼   cup olive oil
1   small onion, chopped
1   small carrot, chopped
1   stalk celery, chopped
6   cloves garlic, peeled and crushed

1   tsp. coarsely crushed whole
      black peppercorn
1   sprig thyme
1   sprig rosemary
4   cups cabernet sauvignon
4   cups Brown Beef Stock (see pg. 146)

In a large sauce pan heat the oil over medium-high heat. Add the onion, carrot, celery, garlic, thyme, rosemary and peppercorn. Sauté for about 8 minutes or until the vegetables are golden brown. Deglaze with the wine, and reduce the liquid by two-thirds (to about 1½ cups). Add the Brown Beef Stock and again reduce by two-thirds. Strain through a fine mesh sieve into a clean pan, and continue to reduce until the sauce is thick enough to coat the back of a spoon.

# BEEF WELLINGTON

Serves 4

For the duxelle

| | | | | |
|---|---|---|---|---|
| ¼ | lb. shiitake mushrooms, stemmed and finely chopped | 2 | Tbs. olive oil |
| ¼ | lb. cremini mushrooms, finely chopped | 2 | Tbs. shallots, finely chopped |
| ¼ | lb. oyster mushrooms, finely chopped | 1 | tsp. garlic, minced |
| | | 1½ | Tbs. brandy |
| | | ½ | cup heavy cream |
| | | ½ | tsp. fresh thyme, chopped |
| | | | Coarse salt and pepper to taste |

2   oz. foie gras, cut into 4 pieces (liver pate may be used)

1   tsp. canola oil or pan searing

For the pastry

1   sheet puff pastry

1   egg. lightly beaten

1   Tbs. milk

For the meat

4   6 oz. beef tenderloins, well trimmed

1   Tbs. canola oil

Coarse salt and ground black pepper

1   cup Cabernet Sauvignon Sauce (see pg. 118)

For the mushroom mixture, heat the oil in a large sauté pan over medium-high heat. Add the shallots and garlic and sauté briefly, 20 seconds. Add the mushrooms and sauté until all liquid of mushrooms is evaporated. Deglaze with brandy. Add the heavy cream, thyme and salt and pepper. Reduce the cream, stirring occasionally until mixture becomes pasty. Remove from heat to cool.

In a non-stick pan with very little oil, sear the foie gras very quickly. Remove from the pan. Set aside.

Preheat the oven to 400 degrees.

For the meat, heat the oil in a large saucepan over high heat. Season the fillets with salt and pepper and add to pan. Sear for 2 minutes and turn over for another 2 minutes. Remove from heat. Set aside to cool.

For the pastry, roll puff pastry ⅛ inch thick. Cut the sheet into 4 squares. In the center of each pastry place the foie gras. Divide the duxelle and top over the foie gras and then top with fillet. Brush the ends of puff pastry with egg. Fold the corner of pastry over the fillet and press all the seams together to seal it well. Turn the fillet over and place on parchment lined sheet pan. Brush pastry with egg mixture. Decorate with strips of pastry, or with circles, and bake it in the oven for 15 minutes.

Transfer the Wellington to individual plates and spoon sauce around it.

## CORIANDER *and* PEPPER SEARED TUNA          Serves 4

| | |
|---|---|
| 1½ lb. 4–6 oz. yellow fin tuna loin steaks, no skin or bloodline | ½ cup Mango and Pineapple salsa, (see pg. 48) |
| 2 Tbs. coriander seeds, crushed | ½ cup Ginger-Soy Sauce |
| 2 Tbs. black peppercorn, cracked | ¼ cup Wasabi Sauce |
| 2 Tbs. canola oil | Coarse salt to taste |

In a large non-stick sauté pan, heat the oil over high heat. Season the tuna steaks with salt, coriander and peppercorn on both sides.

Add the tuna steaks to pan and sear briefly on both sides to rare, about 1–2 minutes all together. Transfer the tuna to the plates. Top the tuna with Pineapple Mango Salsa and spoon Ginger-Soy Sauce and Wasabi Sauce around the tuna steaks.

Variations: This fish mixes well with sticky rice and Asian vegetables (like baby bok choy).

## WASABI SAUCE          Makes ½ Cup

¼   cup wasabi powder
½   cup cold water

In a small mixing bowl combine Wasabi powder and cold water and whisk thoroughly. Refrigerate when not in use. It can last for several weeks well covered in an airtight container.

## GINGER SOY SAUCE          Makes 1½ Cups

| | |
|---|---|
| 2 tsp. canola oil | ¼ cup dry sherry wine |
| 2 tsp. sesame seed oil | 1½ cups light soy sauce |
| 1 Tbs. garlic, minced | ⅓ cup brown sugar |
| 1 Tbs. fresh ginger, peeled and minced | Juice of 1 lime |
| | 1 Tbs. corn starch |
| | 1 Tbs. cold water |

In a small saucepan heat the canola and sesame oil over medium-high heat. Add the garlic and ginger, stir and sauté briefly, about 1 minute. Deglaze with sherry wine. Add in soy sauce, brown sugar and lime juice. Bring to boil. Lower the heat to simmer for 5 minutes.

Meanwhile in a small cup mix the cornstarch and water and pour into sauce to lightly thicken. Strain through fine mesh sieve.

## CHOP HOUSE SALAD                                    Serves 4

1   head green romaine, rinsed and dried
2   qts. mesclun (mixed baby greens)
½   small head iceberg lettuce,
      trimmed and cored
1   beefsteak tomato, cut into wedges
1   cup shiitake mushrooms,
      stemmed and cut in half
1   cup cremini mushrooms, cut in half

1   cup Roquefort cheese dressing,
      or any other bleu cheese dressing
2   Tbs. olive oil
½   tsp. fresh thyme, chopped
½   cup Roquefort cheese chunks
½   cup scallions, chopped,
      green and white part
1   12-oz. New York strip steak, well trimmed
    Coarse salt and pepper to taste

In a sauté pan, heat 1 Tbs. of oil over medium-high heat. Add the mushrooms and sauté until soft, 4 minutes. Season with salt, pepper and thyme. Set aside.

In another sauté pan, heat remaining oil over medium-high heat. Season the steak with salt and pepper and add to pan to sear for 3–4 minutes. Turn over and repeat process. Remove the steak and set aside.

Slice the iceberg into large shreds and chop crosswise. De-rib the head of romaine and then tear into bite size pieces. Place the greens in a large bowl, along with roasted mushrooms, tomatoes and dressing. Toss gently to combine and divide among the plates.

Slice the steak and top over the salads. Sprinkle with crumbled Roquefort bleu cheese and scallions.

## COWBOY STEAK
## *with* RED CHILE ONION RINGS

This particular cut of meat is from beef rib eye loin with bone well trimmed (frenched). I've always been a fan of rib eye steaks because they're easy to cook and packed with flavor.

For the beef

4   18–20 oz. Rib Eye steaks, 1½-inch thick, room temperature
    Coarse salt and finely ground pepper

For the salsa

1   small red onion, finely diced
1   lb. tomatoes, cut into ¼-inch pieces
3   Tbs. fresh lime juice
3   Tbs. fresh cilantro, finely chopped
1   jalapeno chile pepper, seeded and finely chopped
1   Tbs. olive oil
    Salt to taste

For the onion rings

| | | | |
|---|---|---|---|
| 2 | large white onions, cut into ⅙–⅛ inch wide rings (yellow onion may be used) | 1 | Tbs. cornstarch |
| | | 1½ | tsp. salt |
| | | 1½ | tsp. ground cumin |
| 1½ | cup milk | 1 | tsp. sugar |
| 1½ | cups all-purpose flour | 1 | tsp. Hungarian hot paprika |
| ¼ | cup chili powder | 1 | qt. canola oil for frying |

For the salsa, soak red onion in water in large bowl for 30 minutes. Drain thoroughly. Transfer to medium bowl. Add tomatoes, lime juice, cilantro, chili pepper, oil and salt and toss well. Cover salsa with plastic wrap and refrigerate until ready to serve (this can be prepared 4 hours ahead).

For the onion rings, soak onions in milk in a large bowl for 1 hour. Drain thoroughly. Mix all remaining ingredients except for oil in another large bowl. Dredge onion in flour mixture; shake off excess. Heat oil in large heavy sauce pan to 370 degrees. Add onion in batches and cook until golden brown, about 45 seconds. Transfer to paper towels using a slotted spoon; drain well and keep warm.

Meanwhile, prepare barbeque over medium-high heat. Season steak with salt and pepper and grill to desired doneness (about 7 minutes per side for medium rare). Transfer to plates. Drain salsa and spoon onto steaks. Serve steaks with onion rings.

## CRAB *and* LOBSTER CAKES        Serves 4 (eight 6-oz. cakes)

Crab and lobster cakes don't have to be hard to make. Actually, the more you tinker with them, the more you take away from their subtle flavor. At the Chop House we like using pasteurized Jumbo lump crab meat. It is always available, ready to use, and safe to eat. Besides, once it's made into cakes, you'll be hard-pressed tasting the difference between fresh and pasteurized. Left unopened, pasteurized crabmeat can last up to 30 days in your refrigerator. Once opened, use within 2 days.

| | | | |
|---|---|---|---|
| 1 | lb. lump crabmeat, drained | 2 | tsp. coarse salt |
| 1 | lb. cooked lobster meat, cut into ¼–½ inch chunks | 2 | Tbs. chopped parsley |
| | | 1 | Tbs. fresh tarragon, chopped |
| 1½ | cups Panko bread crumbs | 2 | Tbs. unsalted butter |
| 3 | eggs | 2 | Tbs. shallots, finely chopped |
| ⅔ | cup mayonnaise | ½ | cup red peppers, seeded, finely chopped |
| 1 | Tbs. dijon mustard | 4 | scallions, minced |
| 1 | Tbs. lemon juice | 4 | Tbs. canola oil |
| 1 | Tbs. Worcestershire sauce | 1 | cup Roasted Red Pepper Coulis (see pg. 130) |
| ½ | tsp. cayenne | ⅓ | cup Basil Oil (see pg. 86) |

In a small sauté pan, melt butter over medium- high heat. Add the peppers and shallots and sauté until soft, about 3–4 minutes. Stir in scallions. Remove from heat to cool the mixture.

In a large mixing bowl, combine lobster, crabmeat and Panko bread crumbs; set aside.

In a separate large mixing bowl, whisk together eggs, mayonnaise, Dijon mustard, Worcestershire, lemon juice, cayenne, tarragon, parsley and salt. Mix in the red pepper mixture. Combine crab and lobster mixture with wet ingredients using rubber spatula to keep crabmeat intact. Form the cakes and transfer to a parchment lined baking sheet. Chill 1 hour.

### Cooking the cakes

To cook the crab and lobster cakes, all you're shooting for is to fry them to a golden brown. This gives the eggs plenty of time to cook and bind. For best frying results, keep in mind three rules: 1) Use a non-stick pan—you don't want the delicate cake sticking. 2) Sauté in plain vegetable oil. Other fats taste too strong. 3) Don't overcrowd the pan. This way it can maintain its heat when the cakes are added and it's easier to turn them over with a spatula.

In a large non-stick pan, heat the oil over medium-high heat. Add the cakes in batches so the pan isn't crowded. Sauté until golden brown, about 4–5 minutes per side. Drain on paper towels and hold in 200 degree oven if necessary.

Transfer the cakes to individual plates and spoon the Roasted Red Pepper Coulis and Basil Oil around the cakes.

**Variation:** You may omit the Roasted Red Pepper Coulis and Basil Oil and use Tartar, Remoulade or Mustard Sauce to accommodate your personal taste.

## CREAMY FOREST MUSHROOM SOUP    Serves 8–10

Soups are marvelous starters that transcend the season. There is nothing better than to
  begin a winter meal with a hearty, rich, hot soup that sets the stage for the dishes to follow.

| | | | |
|---|---|---|---|
| ¼ | cup olive oil | ⅔ | cup dry sherry wine |
| ½ | lb. shallots, finely chopped | 3 | cups Chicken Stock (see pg. 147) |
| 2 | Tbs. garlic, minced | 4 | cups porcini stock |
| 1 | lb. shiitake mushrooms, stemmed and sliced | 3 | cups heavy cream |
| | | 2 | tsp. fresh thyme, chopped |
| 1 | lb. cremini mushrooms, sliced | 2 | Tbs. unsalted butter |
| 5 | oz. dry porcini mushrooms | 2 | Tbs. fresh chives, finely chopped |
| | | | Coarse salt and pepper to taste |

Soak the dry porcini mushrooms in 4 cups of warm water for 30 minutes. Drain the
  mushrooms. Set aside and reserve the stock.

In a large sauce pan heat the oil over medium-high heat until hot but not smoking. Sauté
  mushrooms, shallots and garlic, stirring until liquid mushroom gives off is completely
  evaporated and mushrooms begin to brown. Reserve ⅔ cup of the sautéed mushroom.
  Set aside keeping warm. This will be used as a garnish later on.

Add sherry wine and boil, stirring occasionally, until liquid is evaporated. Stir in mushroom
  stock, Chicken Stock and thyme and bring to a boil. Stir in cream, salt and pepper and
  simmer uncovered for 15 minutes.

In a blender puree soup in batches until smooth (use caution when blending hot liquids),
  transfer to a sauce pan and reheat over moderately low heat until hot. Whisk in butter
  until all is incorporated. Serve soup garnished with chives and sautéed mushrooms.

## ROASTED RED PEPPER COULIS    Makes about 1 cup

| | |
|---|---|
| 3 | red bell peppers, roasted, peeled and seeded |
| 1 | Tbs. olive oil |
| 1½ | tsp. balsamic vinegar |
| ¼ | tsp. ground cumin |
| 1½ | tsp. salt |
| ½ | tsp. ground black pepper |

Cut the roasted peppers into small pieces and puree with remaining ingredients in a blender.

If using a grill, place the peppers over medium-hot coals, turning them as the skin blackens
  and blisters 10–15 minutes. Remove immediately to avoid over cooking the flesh. If using a
  broiler, place the peppers on a rack positioned about 6 inches from the pre-heated source
  of heat and turn frequently to blacken all sides. If using a gas burner, place the peppers
  on the burner rack directly over the flame and proceed in the same fashion. Adjust the
  heat if necessary or raise the peppers away from the flame by stacking 2 racks together.

Transfer the roasted peppers to a large bowl and cover tightly with plastic wrap. Let them
  steam for 10–15 minutes. Using a small knife, cut away the stems, open the peppers up
  and remove the seeds and membranes. Wipe the work surface clean with a damp towel
  whenever necessary. Scrape away the charred skin.

## GREEK SALAD

| | | | |
|---|---|---|---|
| 1 | head green romaine lettuce, rinsed and diced | 2 | large tomatoes cut into wedges |
| 3 | qts. mixed baby greens | 4 | scallions or red onions, thinly sliced |
| 12 | sliced red beets | 8 | pepperoncini |
| 1 | small seedless cucumber, peeled and cut into ⅛-inch slices | ⅓ | cup calamata olives, preferably pitted |
| | | 1 | cup feta cheese, in ½-inch cubes |
| | | 1 | cup Greek Salad Dressing |

In a large salad bowl, toss the romaine and mixed greens with dressing. Divide the tossed greens evenly among four plates and top with beets slices, cucumber, scallions, pepperoncini, calamata olives, and feta cheese.

## GREEK DRESSING

| | | | |
|---|---|---|---|
| ¼ | cup red wine vinegar | ½ | tsp. fresh rosemary, minced |
| ¼ | cup fresh lemon juice | ½ | tsp. fresh thyme, minced |
| ½ | cup extra virgin olive oil | ½ | tsp. fresh oregano, minced |
| 1 | Tbs. sugar | | Pinch crushed red pepper flakes |
| 1 | Tbs. garlic, minced | | Coarse salt to taste |

In a mixing bowl combine all ingredients and whisk well. If using dried herbs, be sure they were purchased within the last six months for freshness and cut back to ¼ tsp. each.

# GRILLED PORK CHOPS

Serves 4

For brine

6    garlic cloves
⅓    cup coarse salt
¼    cup black peppercorn
¼    cup sugar
1    Tbs. fresh thyme, coarsely chopped
½    tsp. whole allspice
1    bay leaf

For the chops

8    7-oz. pork chops, well trimmed
½    cup olive oil
1    Tbs. garlic, minced
2    Tbs. fresh rosemary
     Coarse salt and pepper to taste

Lightly mash garlic with flat side of a large heavy knife. In a sauce pan, bring 2 quarts of
    water to a boil with garlic and remaining ingredients and simmer for 15 minutes. Cool
    brine completely.

Working over a bowl, divide pork chops and brine among 2 large heavy sealable plastic bags
    and seal bags, pressing out any excess air. Marinade pork chops in bags in a large bowl.
    Chill, turning them once, for 1 day.

Remove pork chops from brine, discarding brine and any spices still adhering to chops and
    pat dry.

In a small bowl whisk together olive oil, garlic and rosemary. Rub each chop with marinade.

Cooking the chops

Season the chops with salt and pepper.

Grill the chops on a hot oiled rack for 4–5 minutes on each side, or until a meat
    thermometer diagonally inserted 2 inches into centers registers 150 degrees.

Transfer the chops to a platter.

## NEW YORK STRIP STEAK
*with* HERB BUTTER

Nicely marbled, well aged, high heat and simple seasonings are the beginnings of the perfect steak. Cooking a strip steak (known as a New York or Kansas City strip if bone-in) encompasses most steak grilling techniques. Only thick steaks like a 2 inch Porterhouse or Rib steak are cooked differently.

Most steak should be cut ¾ to 1 inch thick. At this thickness, they can be cooked directly over the hot part of the grill. At the chop house, we use 18 oz. Prime strip steak. So they are thicker than 1 inch, about 1½ inch, however prime meat is not available in a retail market.

### For the steaks

4   10–12 oz. New York Strip, well trimmed, room temperature
2   Tbs. canola oil
    Coarse salt and freshly ground black pepper

As the grill heats, brush grate with oil so steak won't stick. Season the steaks generously with salt and pepper, and put on the grill at a 45 degree angle, and cook 2–3 minutes to sear marks on their surface. Rotate the steak 90 degrees and continue grilling for 2–4 minutes. Turn the steaks and repeat the same process. Try to keep the grill lid closed during the cooking.

When done, transfer steaks to platters to rest for 3 minutes. While they sit, top each steak with Herb Butter. Rub the butter over the top of each steak.

### For the Herb Butter

4    Tbs. salted butter, room temperature
1½ Tbs. fresh tarragon, finely chopped, or herb of choice
½   tsp. lemon zest, finely grated
¼   tsp. freshly ground black pepper
    Few drops of lemon juice

In a small mixing bowl, cream the butter, herbs, zest, pepper and juice; mound in center of plastic wrap square. Roll into a cylinder, twisting ends of plastic to seal; chill until firm.

## PEPPER STEAK

| | | | |
|---|---|---|---|
| 4 | 10–12 oz New York Strip steak, trimmed, room temperature | 3 | Tbs. olive oil |
| 4 | Tbs. cracked black pepper, or to taste | ¼ | cup shallots, minced |
| | Coarse salt to taste | ½ | cup brandy |
| | | 1 | cup heavy cream |
| | | ¼ | cup Brown Veal Stock (see pg. 146) |
| | | ¼ | cup Demi Glace (see pg. 146) |

Place the steaks between plastic wrap, and with the flat side of your mallet lightly pound over firm surface.

In a large sauté pan, heat the oil over medium-high heat. Season steaks generously with salt and pepper and press firmly with your hand to adhere.

Add steaks to the pan and cook about 1–2 minutes. Turn the steaks over and continue to cook for additional 2 minutes for medium rare, or to desired doneness. Add the shallots and sauté briefly, making sure not to burn it. Deglaze with brandy. Move the steaks to a warm platter and keep warm. To the pan, add heavy cream, Demi Glaze and Veal Stock. Bring sauce to a boil and reduce to ⅔. Spoon the sauce over the steaks.

# ROASTED RACK OF VENISON

Serves 4–6

For this we use our premium venison, farm raised and grass fed in New Zealand. It is exceptionally lean and tender with a mild and distinctive flavor. It is best served rare.

For the marinade

| | | | |
|---|---|---|---|
| 1 | cup dry red wine | 2 | bay leaves |
| ¼ | cup olive oil | 2 | tsp. black peppercorns |
| 1 | small carrot, coarsely chopped | 5 | fresh thyme sprigs |
| 2 | tsp. whole juniper | 2 | fresh rosemary sprigs |

For the venison sauce (makes 2 cups)

| | | | |
|---|---|---|---|
| 3 | Tbs. olive oil | 1½ | cups dry red wine |
| 3 | Tbs. shallots, minced | ⅓ | cup cider vinegar |
| 1½ | cups fresh cranberries, washed and drained | 1½ | cups Veal Demi Glace (see pg. 146) |
| 2 | tsp. ginger root, peeled and grated | ¼ | cup pure maple syrup |
| | | | Coarse salt and ground pepper |

For the meat

1  40–48 oz. venison rack, trimmed
2  Tbs. olive oil
   Coarse salt and ground pepper

For the marinade, combine all ingredients in a large mixing bowl and pour into a large zip lock bag. Place the rack into marinade and seal the bag. Let stand overnight in refrigerator.

Making the sauce

Preheat oven to 400 degrees.

Remove venison rack from marinade and pat dry. Season with salt and pepper. In a large sauté pan heat olive oil over high heat. Add to the pan venison rack flat (meat) side first. Cook for 3–4 minutes. Turn rack over and cook for an additional 2–3 minutes or until browned. Transfer rack onto a sheet pan.

Drain excess grease and leave the pan on the fire. Add shallots and sauté until soft, 2 minutes. Add the cranberries and ginger and cook, stirring 2 minutes. Add wine and vinegar and cook over high heat, stirring occasionally until liquid is reduced to about half, about 5 minutes.

Add Veal Demi Glace and maple syrup and cook until liquid is reduced to about half, about 3–4 minutes. Season the sauce with salt and pepper and strain through a fine mesh sieve, pressing on solids to extract more flavor. Keep warm.

Cooking the venison rack

Roast the venison in a 400 degree oven for about 8–10 minutes or until internal temperature, when a thermometer inserted in center, reads 125–135 degrees. It must be rare or medium rare to appreciate tenderness.

Let the rack rest for 8–10 minutes before carving. With a sharp knife cut each bone through and transfer onto plates. Spoon sauce around the roasted loin.

## SAUTEED SPINACH

Spinach is inherently tender and doesn't need much time to cook. One great method is to blanch it in boiling water for literally a second or two, then drain it. This helps eliminate the astringency common to spinach. Blanching spinach before sautéing may seem like overkill, but it emphasizes the flavor and texture of this everyday vegetable.

1    lb. spinach, stemmed, washed and drained
3    Tbs. olive oil
4-5 cloves garlic, thinly sliced
¼    tsp. crushed red pepper flakes
       Coarse salt and pepper to taste
       Balsamic vinegar or lemon juice (optional)

To stem spinach, fold the leaf in half at the stem and pull the stem down the length of the leaf. Small leaves can be cooked as they are.

Bring a large pot of water to boil over high heat. Wilt spinach in boiling water. Add it all at once, stir, and drain immediately in a colander. Do not let spinach sit in the water. Press as much liquid from it as possible, forming it into a disk.

Heat the oil in a large sauté pan over medium-high heat. Add garlic and pepper flakes; sauté until garlic turns golden, about 1 minute (do not burn the garlic, it will taste bitter). Stir constantly.

Add the disk of spinach and break it up with a wooden spoon or tongs, stirring to coat with oil and garlic. Cook just until heated through, about 1 minute. Season with salt and pepper then transfer spinach to a serving platter

Drizzle spinach with balsamic vinegar before serving.

## TARTAR SAUCE

Makes 1¼ Cups

| | | | |
|---|---|---|---|
| 1 | cup mayonnaise | 2 | tsp. white wine vinegar |
| 2 | Tbs. pickle relish | 1 | tsp. Dijon mustard |
| 1 | Tbs. capers | 2 | Tbs. chopped fresh parsley |
| 1 | Tbs. onion, grated | | Salt and pepper to taste |

In a mixing bowl whisk all the ingredients.

## REMOULADE SAUCE

Makes 1¼ Cups

| | | | |
|---|---|---|---|
| ½ | cup red bell pepper, seeded and chopped | 2 | Tbs. shallots, chopped |
| ¼ | cup scallions, chopped | 2 | Tbs. chopped fresh parsley |
| ¼ | cup Dijon mustard | 2 | Tbs. honey |
| ¼ | cup mayonnaise | 1 | Tbs. fresh lemon juice |
| | | | Salt and pepper to taste |

Process all ingredients in a food processor fitted with a steel blade until vegetables are
   finely chopped. Season with salt and pepper.

## WHITE BALSAMIC VINIAGRETTE

Makes 1 Cup

¼   cup white balsamic vinegar
⅔   cup extra virgin olive oil
1   Tbs. shallots, minced
    Coarse salt and ground black pepper to taste

In a small mixing bowl combine all ingredients and whisk well. Keep refrigerated up to
   2 weeks.

Note: During service keep vinaigrette at room temperature and shake before using.

## ROASTED GARLIC DRESSING

Makes 2 Cups

3   Tbs. Roasted Garlic Puree (see roasted garlic recipe opposite)
½   cup Balsamic vinegar
1½  cups olive oil
    Coarse salt and ground pepper to taste

In a mixing bowl, combine all ingredients and mix well. Keep refrigerated. You may have to
   re-whisk before using for serving.

## ROASTED GARLIC

20 large garlic cloves, unpeeled (choose fresh heads of garlic
   that are firm and not sprouting)
1 Tbs. water
1 Tbs. extra virgin olive oil
   Coarse salt and freshly ground pepper to taste

Preheat the oven to 325 degrees. Place the garlic in a small baking dish and toss with the oil, water, salt and pepper. Cover with aluminum foil and bake until the garlic is tender (squeeze a clove to check), 25–35 minutes.

Roasted garlic may be prepared up to 2 days in advance, covered and refrigerated.

Slow roasting mellows and sweetens the impact of raw garlic and transforms it into a versatile ingredient, allowing cooks to add a subtle wave of garlic flavor to butters, oils, soups, vinaigrettes, pizza, pasta and sauce.

Roasted Garlic Puree is made by pressing the cooked garlic out of its skin into a bowl and mashing it with a fork. One large head of garlic will yield about 3 Tbs. puree.


## ROQUEFORT CHEESE DRESSING

Blue cheese is the king of dressings, and this is one you must make. Period. The cheese is the star here, so use the best you can find. Steer clear of the pre-crumbled stuff. It tastes stale. At The Chop House we use strictly Roquefort. It is a bit pricey, but it's worth it.

2 cups mayonnaise
1 cup Roquefort cheese chunks
1 cup sour cream
1 tsp. fresh garlic, minced
¼ cup celery, finely diced

3 Tbs. green onions, finely chopped, green part only
2 tsp. fresh lemon juice
   Salt, pepper and Tabasco to taste
2 tsp. white crème de menthe (optional)

In a large mixing bowl, whisk all the ingredients together. Chill at least an hour before serving to allow flavors to blend. If it's too thick, thin it out with a little milk. Keeps for up to one week, chilled.

**Variation:** You may substitute Maytag bleu cheese for Roquefort. It is the best American bleu cheese.

## BROWN BEEF STOCK / VEAL DEMI GLACE

In areas where beef bones are not available, substitute veal bones in equal proportions.

| | | | |
|---|---|---|---|
| 6 | lb. beef bones | 4 | bay leaves |
| 2 | cups onion, chopped | ½ | bunch fresh parsley |
| 2 | cups carrots, chopped | 1 | Tbs. black peppercorn |
| 2 | cups celery, chopped | 6 | oz. canned tomato paste |
| 1 | head of garlic, cut in half | 3 | cups dry red wine |
| 6 | sprigs fresh thyme, or 1 tsp. dried | 1½ | gallon (6 qts) water |

Preheat the oven to 450 degrees. Place the bones in a large roasting pan and bake in the oven until browned on all sides, about 1 hour. With a wooden spoon, apply a coat of tomato paste over the bones for color and bake for an additional 20 minutes. Add the onion, carrots, celery and garlic and bake for 30 minutes more until nicely browned. Remove the roasting pan from the oven and place contents of roaster in a large stockpot and add all ingredients except red wine and water.

Place the roasting pan over high heat on the stove and deglaze with red wine by cooking 4 minutes while scraping to dissolve any hardened brown particles. Pour into the stock pot and add enough water to cover. Bring to a boil. Skim the impurities (blood, fat and albumin). They can cause a cloudy stock. Reduce the heat and simmer for 4–6 hours. Add more water if necessary and let simmer for half an hour after the last addition. After 4–6 hours of slow simmering, the stock is ready. It will be a rich mahogany color.

Remove from the heat, let cool, skim off any fat, and strain the stock into a clean container using a fine mesh strainer. Let the stock drip naturally; if you mash the vegetables, the stock will turn cloudy.

The stock will keep up to one week in the refrigerator, and up to 2 months frozen.

Note: To make demiglace, use veal bones and reduce the stock further by one fourth.

## CHICKEN STOCK

Makes 3 Quarts

Chicken stock is never far from reach in any of our restaurants. In fact, it's hard for me to imagine cooking without it. It is such an important component and flavor ingredient for so many of our dishes. If you do use canned chicken stock instead, be sure to adjust for salt, as most canned stocks are quite salty.

| | | | |
|---|---|---|---|
| 5 | lb. raw chicken wings, backs or necks (or a combination) | 3 | cloves garlic, halved crosswise |
| 1 | cup onion, coarsely chopped | 4-6 | sprigs thyme, or 1 tsp. dried thyme |
| 1 | cup celery, coarsely chopped | 4-6 | sprigs flat leaf parsley |
| 1 | cup carrot, coarsely chopped | 1 | tsp. black peppercorn |
| | | 3 | bay leaves |
| | | 4 | qts. cold water |

Carefully rinse chicken bones to wash off any blood, place the chicken bones in a large stock pot and add cold water to cover by 2 inches. Bring to a boil over high heat, skimming off any foam that rises to the surface. Add the remaining ingredients, reduce the heat to half and simmer uncovered, gently for 3, or up to 6 hours.

Strain the stock into a large bowl and cool completely. Skim off and discard the clear yellow fat that rises to the surface, or refrigerate the stock until the fat chills, about 8 hours or overnight, then scrape it off with a large spoon.

The stock will keep for 3–4 days in the refrigerator, and up to 2 months frozen.

## FISH STOCK

Makes about 1½ quarts

| | | | |
|---|---|---|---|
| 3 | lb. assorted fish bones (frames and heads, gills removed by snapping with kitchen sheers) from white fleshed fish, such as, grouper, cod, halibut, striped bass or flounder. | ¼ | cup chopped leek, white part only, washed |
| | | 4 | garlic cloves, unpeeled and crushed |
| 1 | cup chopped onion | 1 | tsp black peppercorns |
| ¼ | cup chopped celery | 4 | sprigs flat-leaf parsley |
| | | 1 | sprig thyme |
| | | 1½ | qt. water, or as needed |

Using a heavy knife or a cleaver, chop the bones into large pieces. Place them in a large bowl in the sink and wash well with cold water. Drain.

In a large pot, add the fish bones along with all the remaining ingredients and bring to boil, removing any foam that rises to the surface. Reduce the heat to low and simmer for 30 minutes.

Remove from heat and let stand for 20 minutes. Strain the broth into a large bowl or container, cool completely.

The broth may be prepared up to 2 days in advance, cooled, covered and refrigerated or it can be frozen for up to 2–3 months.

Fish stock cooks in much less time than other stocks because the bones are more delicate. Don't be tempted to simmer it longer than 30 minutes or the flavor will become muddled. The real trick to a good fish stock is to rinse the bones well under cold water to refresh their flavor and remove any traces of blood. Don't use bones from oily fleshed fish, such as salmon, bluefish or mackerel.

# La Dolce Vita

— the sweet life — is what you're sure to find

in this distinctive collection of our most

sought-after recipes. Desserts have a special

place on any Mainstreet Ventures menu —

they're the ultimate evening afterglow to a

delightful dining experience. Specialty desserts

are made from scratch using only the finest

ingredients, such as imported Danish chocolate, and fresh seasonal fare. Chef Simon especially recommends the Vanilla Bean Creme Brulee, a popular selection all year round.

We make presentation, another of our hallmarks, an art form — and our pastry chefs are very creative. With a style best-described as eclectic, they often place a contemporary confection, like Frozen Chocolate Soufflé, right beside something very homey and traditional, like bread pudding. But desserts really take center stage at La Dolce Vita, with two Michigan locations dedicated entirely to after-dinner pleasures.

In Ann Arbor, La Dolce Vita is situated between Gratzi and The Chop House, with access from either restaurant. In Grand Rapids, La Dolce Vita is a featured section below The Chop House dining area. Both locations offer comfortable couches surrounding small tables. The setting is perfect for relaxing and enjoying dessert, cappuccino or a world-class selection of after dinner drinks. La Dolce Vita Ann Arbor has its own cigar lounge downstairs where guests can enjoy hand-rolled cigars in an exclusive, club-like atmosphere.

Each La Dolce Vita has a dedicated pastry chef. Like all our chefs, each is highly-skilled, with multiple culinary degrees. They serve a core of four or five items throughout the year, while interspersing a selection of desserts to complement each season. In the fall you'll see lots of apple, pumpkin and cranberry. In the winter, we serve very rich, chocolaty desserts. Then, in the spring, we feature desserts with berries and rhubarb. And, in summer, we provide lighter fare, such as fresh fruit and lemons. Chocolate remains our most popular dessert, though, no matter what the season.

Life is never boring when you take the art of dessert making to its highest form. Experience the afterglow for yourself, as you try these recipes and enjoy your own special taste of La Dolce Vita.

Pastry Chef Cheryl Hanewich

La Dolce Vita, Ann Arbor

## FOSTER SAUCE

1   cup brown sugar
1   cup butter
¼   cup rum

Melt butter and brown sugar in a saucepan over medium heat until sugar is dissolved.
Remove from heat and slowly stir in rum.

## BANANAS FOSTER BREAD PUDDING                    Serves 6

4   large egg yolks                     1   cup brown sugar
½   cup milk                            1½  tsp. cinnamon
1¼ cups heavy cream                     ¼   cup rum
2   medium bananas                      ¾   teaspoon vanilla extract
½   cup sugar                           3   cups bread cubes

Preheat oven to 350 degrees. Brush six, 8-ounce ramekins or custard cups with melted butter.
   Toast bread cubes in oven until light golden brown, about 10 minutes.

Heat milk and cream in a medium saucepan until hot but not boiling.

In a food processor puree egg yolks and bananas until smooth. Alternately you can mash
   bananas and yolks with a fork or masher.

In a large bowl, combine brown sugar, sugar and cinnamon. Add hot milk and banana
   mixture. Mix well to combine. Stir in rum and vanilla extract. Add bread cubes and toss
   well with mixture to coat. Let mixture sit for 15 minutes.

Divide evenly into the six dishes. Place in a roaster pan. Lightly grease a piece of tin foil
   and put greased side down over the pan to cover.

Bake 45 minutes, take off the foil and bake an additional 10 minutes. Cool 15 minutes and
   invert onto plate. Serve with vanilla ice cream and Foster Sauce.

## MELT CAKES

Serves 6

15  oz. of bittersweet chocolate, finely chopped.
1    cup butter
6    eggs

Preheat oven to 350 degrees. Butter and flour six, 8-ounce ramekins or custard cups.

Over a double boiler, melt chocolate and butter, stirring occasionally.

Whip six eggs on a stand mixer until thick, about 5 minutes. Fold the chocolate into the eggs and divide evenly among the ramekins.

Place ramekins in a roasting pan and fill with hot water halfway up the sides of the dishes.

Bake 25 minutes or until just set.

Cool 10 minutes. Run a thin knife around the edge of the cakes. Invert onto serving plate.

Serve with Chocolate Sauce and ice cream.


## CHOCOLATE SAUCE

Makes about 1 cup

8    oz. chocolate
½   cup milk
6    Tbs. butter

Over a pan of simmering water set a bowl with all the ingredients in it. Whisk until chocolate and butter are melted. Pour into a container and cover.

This is an easy, great tasting sauce that will hold for 1 week.

Add 1 tablespoon Grand Marnier, Bailey's, rum, or any flavoring you like to it.

# PEANUT BUTTER TERRINE

### Terrine

| | |
|---|---|
| 12 | oz. of bittersweet chocolate, finely chopped |
| 2 | Tbs. butter |
| ½ | cup smooth peanut butter |
| 4 | large egg yolks |
| ¼ | cup sugar |
| 1½ | cups heavy cream |

### Chocolate Glaze

| | |
|---|---|
| 4 | oz. of bittersweet chocolate, finely chopped |
| 5 | Tbs. butter |
| 2 | tsp. corn syrup |

Line a 9½ x 4 x 3 loaf pan with plastic wrap.

Melt chocolate, butter, and peanut butter over a double boiler.

Combine yolks and sugar in a heat proof bowl over simmering water and whisk until thick.

Whip heavy cream to soft peaks.

Fold yolks and sugar into chocolate and fold in cream. Pour into prepared loaf pan.
   Chill 4 hours.

Melt all ingredients for glaze over a double boiler. When terrine is chilled, unmold
   and pour glaze.

## APPLE CRANBERRY CRISP                    Serves 4

| | |
|---|---|
| 4    cups sliced apples | For crisp topping |
| ⅓    dried cranberries | ¾    cup flour |
| 1    tsp. cinnamon | 1    cup sugar |
| ¼    cup brown sugar | 5½  Tbs. butter |
| ¼    cup water | |

Preheat oven to 350 degrees. Make crisp topping by combining sugar and flour in a bowl.
   Cut butter into mixture using a pastry cutter or your fingertips.

Toss apples and cranberries with cinnamon, brown sugar and water in a large bowl.
   Pour mixture into a 8x8 inch square baking pan.

Cover generously with crisp topping and bake for 40 minutes or until apples are soft.
   Serve with Cinnamon Ice Cream.


## CINNAMON ICE CREAM                    Makes 1½ Quarts

| | |
|---|---|
| 2    cups heavy cream | 2    tsp. cinnamon |
| 2½  cups milk | 2    cinnamon sticks |
| 1    Tbs. vanilla extract | 3    large egg yolks |
| 1    cup sugar | |

Combine milk, cream, vanilla and sugar in a heavy bottomed saucepan and mix well.

Add cinnamon and cinnamon sticks. Bring to a boil.

Temper the egg yolks by adding a little of the hot milk mixture and whisk together.
   Pour yolk mixture into saucepan and cook until slightly thickened.

Strain into a bowl and chill at least 4 hours or overnight.

Freeze in ice cream maker according to manufacturer's directions.


## VANILLA ICE CREAM                    Makes 1½ Quarts

3    cups whole milk
¾    cup heavy cream
1    cup sugar
7    large egg yolks
1½  tsp. vanilla extract

Heat milk and cream in heavy bottomed saucepan over medium heat until hot.

Whisk egg yolks and sugar in a heat proof bowl. Temper the egg yolks by adding a little of
   the hot milk and whisk together. Add yolk mixture back into pan and cook over low heat
   until slightly thickened.

Strain mixture into a bowl and stir in vanilla extract. Chill mixture in refrigerator for at least
   4 hours or overnight.

Freeze in an ice cream maker according to manufacturer's directions.

## TIRAMISU

1   lb. mascarpone cheese
4   oz. pasteurized egg yolks
½   cup sugar
2   Tbs. brandy (optional)
4   oz. frozen pasteurized egg whites (thawed)
1   pkg. ladyfingers
1½ cup espresso or very strong coffee
   Cocoa powder

In a large bowl combine yolks and sugar, whisk until thick. Add brandy and mix into yolks.

Add mascarpone cheese and mix to combine.

Whip egg whites in mixer until stiff peaks form. Fold whites into mascarpone custard.

Quickly dip ladyfingers in espresso and lay in pan in 2 neat rows, filling the bottom with the biscuits. Pour ½ the mascarpone custard on top of the biscuits and spread evenly.

Pour some cocoa powder in a sifter and cover the top of the custard.

Dip lady fingers in espresso and lay on top in a second layer.

Pour rest of custard on top and spread evenly.

Dust with more cocoa to cover.

Wrap pan in plastic wrap and freeze overnight.

To serve, thaw in refrigerator ½ hour. Remove, cut serving size while still slightly frozen. May be left in pan until served or put on dessert plate and chilled until served. Garnish with chocolate sauce and chocolate shavings.

Note: Tiramisu, which means "pick me up" in Italian, is wonderful with a cup of espresso in the afternoon to get you through the rest of the day like the Italians do!

## GINGER PUMPKIN PUDDING CAKES

Makes 6

4    Tbs. butter
2    oz. fresh ginger, coarsely chopped
½    cup molasses
½    tsp. baking soda
1¼   cups flour
1    tsp. ground ginger
½    tsp. ground cinnamon
¼    tsp. ground nutmeg
1½   tsp. baking powder
⅔    cup brown sugar
1    egg
1    cup pumpkin puree

Preheat oven to 350 degrees.

Using vegetable spray, lightly grease 6 mini bundt pans, set aside.

Place ginger in saucepan with 1 cup hot water. Simmer until reduced to ½ cup. Remove from heat, strain, add molasses and baking soda to liquid and set aside.

Mix together dry ingredients.

In mixer, cream butter and sugar together. Add egg and mix well. Add pumpkin puree.

Add dry ingredients alternately with the molasses mixture. Scrape bowl.

Fill bundt pans halfway with batter. Bake about 18–20 minutes until firm.

Invert pans to release cakes.

Note: These little cakes are a great fall favorite. Dress them up with a dollop of whipped cream and some Caramel Sauce.

## CARAMEL SAUCE

1½   cups brown sugar
1    cup corn syrup
½    cup butter
1    cup heavy cream

In a heavy saucepan over medium-high heat, combine brown sugar, corn syrup and butter.

Stir occasionally to mix ingredients.

Using a thermometer, boil to 240 degrees.

Turn off heat and very slowly add the cream. The mixture will be very hot.

Whisk until mixture is smooth.

Cool completely and store in a covered container.

Note: This easy sauce tastes wonderful over desserts or ice cream. If it becomes too thick, microwave for 30 seconds to warm it up.

## MIXED BERRY CRISP   Makes one 8x8 inch pan, serves 4–6

Topping

1   cup brown sugar
¾   cup flour
¾   cup quick cooking oatmeal
1   tsp. cinnamon
1   tsp. nutmeg
½   cup butter, chilled, cut into small pieces
¼   cup sugar
2   Tbs. all-purpose flour

Filling

4   cups strawberries sliced in half
1¼   cups blueberries
1   cup raspberries

Preheat oven to 350 degrees.

Make topping: Combine brown sugar, flour, cinnamon, and nutmeg in a bowl.

Cut butter into dry ingredients with fingers to break up butter.

Mix in oatmeal and set aside.

Mix ¼ cup sugar and 2 Tbs. flour together.

Combine berries in baking pan and toss with flour and sugar mixture.

Sprinkle topping over berries.

Bake about 30–40 minutes until fruit juices bubble and topping is lightly browned.

Serve warm with vanilla ice cream.

Note: This is a great summer picnic dessert. Use any combination of your favorite summer berries.

## FROZEN CHOCOLATE SOUFFLE

¾ cup heavy cream
¼ cup heavy cream
6 oz. bittersweet chocolate
1 egg
2 egg yolks
3 Tbs. sugar

Have ready six 4-oz. custard cups.

Whip ¾ cup cream and put in refrigerator.

Place a bowl over a pan of simmering water and put ¼ cream and chocolate to melt, stirring often, when melted set aside to cool.

Over the same pan of water, set a bowl with egg, yolks and sugar on top. Whisk until mixture is thick.

Pour thickened eggs into cooled chocolate and mix well.

Add whipped cream and fold in gently.

Pour into dishes and freeze 4–6 hours.

Note: This is an easy "do ahead" dessert that can be garnished with whipped cream, chocolate sauce and berries.

# KEY LIME PIE

Crust

| | |
|---|---|
| 1 | cup graham cracker crumbs |
| 1 | Tbs. sugar |
| 6 | Tbs. melted butter |
| 1 | 9-inch pie pan |

Filling

| | |
|---|---|
| 6 | egg yolks |
| 1 | 13-oz. can sweetened condensed milk |
| ⅔ | cup Key West lime juice |

Preheat oven to 325 degrees.

Combine crumbs, sugar and melted butter. Press on bottom and sides of a 9-inch pie pan. Bake 10 minutes.

Meanwhile make filling.

Whisk yolks. Add condensed milk and whisk to combine. Add lime juice and mix well.

Pour into hot shell and bake 15 minutes.

Cool to room temperature and then chill 2–3 hours.

Can be topped with sweetened whipped cream and lime zest.

Note: This is a classic Key Lime Pie that will have you feeling the island breeze with every bite!

## STRAWBERRY RHUBARB TART

Makes 1 Tart

1    9-inch Sugar Cookie Tart Dough, unbaked

Streusel topping

7    Tbs. unsalted butter, chilled, cut into small pieces
½    cup sugar
1    cup flour
¾    cup ground almonds

1    lb. rhubarb, cut in 1-inch pieces
½    lb. strawberries, cut in half
¾    cup orange juice
     Zest of 1 orange
2    Tbs. butter
1    cup strawberries, cut in half
2    Tbs. sugar
3    Tbs. flour

Preheat oven to 350 degrees.

Make the topping:

Combine ½ cup sugar, 1 cup flour, ¾ cup almonds and mix in 7 Tbs. butter until crumbly; set aside.

In a heavy saucepan, combine rhubarb, ½ lb. sliced strawberries, orange juice, zest and butter. Cook over medium heat until rhubarb is just tender, 4–5 minutes. Cool.

Strain rhubarb and strawberry mixture. Add 1 cup strawberries.

Combine 2 Tbs. sugar with 3 Tbs. flour and sprinkle on bottom of tart shell.

Add filling and sprinkle on topping.

Bake 35–40 minutes until crust is brown and topping is golden.

Cool completely and serve with vanilla ice cream.

Note: A great tart for people who think they don't like rhubarb!

## SUGAR COOKIE TART DOUGH

Makes one 9-inch dough

¼    cup sugar
½    cup butter
1¼   cups flour

Cream the butter and the sugar.

Add flour and mix until dough comes together.

Flatten into disk, wrap in plastic wrap and chill until needed.

Note: A great all-purpose dough—I make my crème pies and fruit pies in this dough.

## BERRIES AND CREAM TORTE

4   cups heavy cream
¼   cup powdered sugar
1   vanilla sponge cake
1   pint strawberries
½   pint raspberries
½   pint blueberries

In a chilled mixing bowl combine cream and sugar, whip until stiff.

Place one cake layer on a plate and spread a thin layer of whipped cream on top.

Slice strawberries thin and place on top of cake, add blueberries and raspberries.

Spread a thin layer of whipped cream over berries, covering them completely.

Use remaining cream to frost the top and sides of cake.

Decorate the sides and top with leftover berries. Chill 1 hour.

Note: Using a serrated knife to gently "saw" each slice works nicely.

## VANILLA SPONGE CAKE

1½ cups all-purpose flour
1½ tsp. baking powder
½   tsp. salt
3   eggs

1½ cups sugar
¾   cup milk
3   Tbs. butter
1½ tsp. vanilla extract

Preheat oven to 350 degrees.

Grease and flour two 9-inch cake pans and line with parchment paper cut to fit the bottom.

Combine flour, baking powder and salt, set aside.

In a saucepan over low heat, combine milk and butter; heat until milk is hot and butter
  is melted.

Using the mixer with the paddle attachment, beat eggs for 3–4 minutes.

Gradually add sugar and continue mixing for 2–3 minutes until thick.

On low speed add flour mixture—mix until just combined. Scrape sides and bottom of bowl.

Stir hot milk and butter and vanilla into batter; mix well.

Pour batter into prepared pan.

Bake 20–25 minutes until cake is lightly golden on top and a toothpick comes out clean.

Cool in pans 15 minutes then turn out onto a cooling rack to completely cool before using.

Note: Once you make this cake, you'll see how easy it is and how great it tastes. It is very
  adaptable and can be used with any filling or frosting.

# CHEESECAKE

### Crust

1   cup graham cracker crumbs
2   Tbs. sugar
4   Tbs. melted butter

Combine ingredients and press into bottom of springform pan.

Have ready a piece of aluminum foil large enough to fold in half, and wrap around the bottom and up the sides of the springform pan.

Preheat the oven to 325 degrees.

### Filling

4   8-oz packages cream cheese(at room temperature)
1½ cups sugar
4   eggs
¼   cup sour cream
¼   cup heavy cream
1   Tbs. vanilla extract

Mix the cream cheese until soft and smooth. Add the sugar and mix, scraping the sides and bottom often. Add the eggs, one at a time.

Combine sour cream, cream and vanilla and add to the cream cheese. Scrape sides and bottom of bowl.

Pour batter into prepared pan. Set pan on cookie sheet and fill with one inch of hot water.

Bake about 1 hour, until firm. When done, remove from water bath and let cool to room temperature. Chill in refrigerator over night.

To remove from pan, take off aluminum foil, unhook pan latch, gently slip a large knife under the crust and slide onto a serving plate. Garnish with whipped cream, sauce or berries.

### Variations

Raspberry

Combine 1 pint raspberries pureed with 2 Tbs. sugar and 2 Tbs. cornstarch. Add to the batter last or after batter is in pan, pour in a circular pattern over the cheesecake. Using a toothpick or small knife, swirl through the batter. Bake as directed.

Coconut

Add ½ cup cream of coconut (such as Coco Lopez) to batter as last ingredient. Pour batter into pan and sprinkle with ¾ cup sweetened coconut on top. Bake as directed.

# VANILLA BEAN CRÈME BRULEE

Makes 4 servings

1½ cups heavy cream
½   cup milk
4   Tbs. sugar, divided
6   egg yolks
½   vanilla bean or 1½ tsp. vanilla extract

Preheat oven to 325 degrees.

Have ready four 8 oz. custard cups, a roasting pan and 1 piece of aluminum foil large
    enough to cover the pan.

In a saucepan, over medium heat, combine milk, cream, 2 Tbs. sugar and vanilla bean split,
    with seeds scraped into liquid. Heat mixture to just scalding.

Combine 2 Tbs. sugar and 6 yolks.

Add some hot milk to yolks and sugar and whisk together.

Pour back into saucepan and cook until slightly thickened.

Strain into a bowl and divide custard into cups and place in roasting pan.

Add enough very hot water to bring it ⅓ of the way up the sides of custard cups.
    Cover with aluminum foil.

Bake about 35–45 minutes—custard should still jiggle slightly but be firm.

Remove from oven and cool.

Chill in refrigerator 2–3 hours.


To "Brulee"

At La Dolce Vita, we use "Sugar in the Raw" because it makes the best caramelized top.

Sprinkle about 1 Tbs. sugar to coat the top of the custard. Place under broiler until sugar
    dissolves and starts to brown or caramelize. Serve immediately as is or garnish with
    fresh fruit.

**Note:** This is our #1 best seller at La Dolce Vita—smooth, creamy, rich, the best!

## CHOCOLATE CREPE *with* WHITE CHOCOLATE MOUSSE FILLING

Makes about 10–12 crepes

White chocolate mousse

| | |
|---|---|
| 2 | cups heavy cream |
| 4 | egg whites |
| ½ | cup sugar |
| 8 | oz. melted white chocolate |
| 4 | oz. finely chopped white chocolate |

Whip heavy cream to soft peaks, store in refrigerator until needed.

Over a pan of simmering water, place a bowl of coarsely chopped white chocolate to melt, stirring often. When melted, set aside.

Over the same pan of water, after chocolate is melted, combine the sugar and egg whites in a clean bowl and whisk together until sugar is melted and egg whites are warm.

Place whites and sugar in the mixer and whip until thick and stiff, about 5–7 minutes.

Combine melted chocolate over whipped whites and fold in. Add whipped cream and finely chopped chocolate and fold in.

Chill for 2 hours.

Crepes

| | |
|---|---|
| ⅔ | cup flour |
| ½ | cup unsweetened cocoa powder, sifted |
| 3 | Tbs. sugar |
| 3 | eggs |
| 1¼ | cups milk |
| 2 | Tbs. melted butter |

Combine flour, cocoa and sugar in a food processor. Pulse to mix.

Add eggs, milk and melted butter. Process 1 minute, scrape the sides and process 10 seconds more. Put crepe batter in bowl and let rest 10 minutes.

Lightly spray an 8 inch frying pan with vegetable cooking spray and place on medium heat.

Pour ¼ cup batter into pan, tilting pan to coat only the bottom of pan. Place back on heat, cook 1 minute, flip crepe over and cook 45 seconds more.

Transfer crepe to a plate. Repeat procedure with the remaining batter.

Stack crepes between parchment or wax paper so they do not stick together.

To serve

Place a chocolate crepe on a plate; add a generous scoop of White Chocolate Mousse on lower half of crepe, fold crepe over the White Chocolate Mousse. Serve with fresh raspberry sauce and a mint leaf.

Note: This is a signature dessert from Gratzi (our sister restaurant next door) which was brought over when La Dolce Vita opened. Our guests love it!

## CARAMEL NUT TART

1   recipe Sugar Cookie Tart Dough (see pg. 170) pressed into a
        9-inch removable bottom tart pan and chilled until needed.
3   cups nuts—use your favorite nuts
        (walnuts, pecans, pistachio, macadamias, etc.)
½   cup butter
1   cup brown sugar
½   cup honey
½   cup heavy cream

Preheat oven to 350 degrees.

Line the tart dough with aluminum foil or wax paper and fill with 2 cups pie weights or
    raw rice.

Bake about 15 minutes, remove weights and bake until dough is very lightly brown,
    about 5 minutes.

For filling

In a heavy sauce pan combine butter, brown sugar and honey. Cook over medium heat until
    melted and slightly caramel in color.

Add nuts and cream and cook 2 minutes longer.

Pour into warm shell and bake 20–25 minutes until bubbly and nicely caramel in color.

Cool and serve with chocolate sauce or vanilla ice cream.

Note: This is the tart for anyone who loves caramel and nuts. Any combination of nuts
    works—use a mixture that you love!

## CHOCOLATE PROFITEROLES    Makes 16–18 profiteroles

1    cup flour
¼    cup unsweetened cocoa, sifted
¾    cup water
2    Tbs. sugar
6    Tbs. butter
4    eggs

Preheat oven to 400 degrees.

Combine flour and cocoa.

In a heavy saucepan, combine water, sugar and butter and bring to a boil.

Reduce heat to low.

Add flour and cocoa, stirring with a wooden spoon until mixture forms a smooth paste and pulls away in a ball from the sides of the pan.

Transfer dough to mixer with paddle and add eggs one at a time until combined.

Drop by teaspoonfuls onto parchment paper lined sheet tray.

Bake 15 minutes, reduce heat to 350 degrees and bake an additional 10–15 minutes until puffs are dry and firm.

Cool completely, cut in half horizontally and fill with your favorite ice cream. Serve 2 or 3 on a plate with chocolate sauce.

# Wine & Cigars

On the following pages we have selected some of our favorite wines that truly complement the recipes in the book. These featured wines are paired with the recipes, by section, to complete your dining experience.

In addition, we have provided a selection of top-notch cigars. If you're in search of the perfect cigar to top off your meal, check out our selections.

## SEAFOOD

*Wine Pairings*

**Parmesan Crusted Sole**  *pg. 46*

Valinor, Albarino,
Rias Baixas, 2002

Elk Cove, Pinot Gris,
Willamette Valley, 2003

Domaine Seguinot, Chablis,
"Vielles Vignes", 2001

**Sauteed Whitefish**  *pg. 50*

Domaine Chandon,
Blanc de Noir, Carneros, NV

Champalou, Vouvray, 2002

Villa Maria, Chardonnay,
Marlborough, 2003

**Stuffed Flounder**  *pg. 58*

Pierre Spaar, Pinot Gris,
"Reserve", Alsace, 2002

Ninth Island, Pinot Noir,
Tasmania, 2003

Cakebread, Chardonnay,
Napa Valley, 2001

**Broiled Scallops**  *pg. 24*

Joh. Jos. Prum,
Riesling Kabinett,
Wehlehner Sonnenuhr, 2002

Batasiolo, Moscato D'Asti, 2003

Chateau Grand Traverse,
Pinot Gris, Old Mission
Penninsula, 2003

**Cioppino** *pg. 26*

Hippolyte Reverdy,
Sancerre, 2003

J. M. Boillot,
Puligny-Montrachet, 2001

Gabbiano, Chianti Classico,
2000

**Paella** *pg. 40*

Vieux Telegraphe,
Chateauneuf-Du-Pape, 2001

Dr. Pauly Bergweiler,
Riesling Spatlese, 2002

Remoissenet et Fil,
Corton Charlemagne, 1996

**Honey Barbecued Salmon** *pg. 28*

Testarossa, Pinot Noir,
"Gary's Vineyard",
Santa Lucia Highlands, 2001

Torbreck, "The Steading",
Barossa Valley, 2001

Calera, Viognier,
Mt. Harlan, 2002

**Dover Sole Meuniere
or Amandine** *pg. 42*

Champalou, Vouvray, 2002

Selene, Sauvignon Blanc,
"Hyde Vineyard", Carneos, 2001

Gary Farrell, Chardonnay,
"Westside Vineyard",
Russian River Valley, 2001

**Linguine with Clams** *pg. 30*

Jackson Estate,
Sauvignon Blanc, Marlborough,
2003

Conundrum, California, 2002

Rochioli, Chardonnay, Russian
River Valley, 2002

**Pan Roasted Chilean Sea Bass** *pg. 44*

MerSoleil, Chardonnay,
Central Coast, 2001

Jermann, Pinot Grigio, Venezie
Giulia, 2003

Ferrari-Carano, "Fume Blanc,
Sonoma County, 2003

## ITALIAN

*Wine Pairings*

**Pollo Al Marsala con Fungi**  *pg. 98*

Monsanto, Chianti Classico
Riserva, 1999

Dutton-Goldfield,
Chardonnay, "Dutton Ranch",
Russian River Valley, 2002

Michelle Chiarlo,
Barbera D'Asti, 2000

**Linguine Del Golfo**  *pg. 90*

Pieropan, Soave Classico
Superiore, 2002

Caputo, Lacryma Christi
Bianco Del Vesuvio, 2003

Cerreto, Arneis,
"Blange", 2003

**Fileto di Manzo**  *pg. 82*

Mastrojanni, Brunello Di
Montalcino, 1997

Marchese di Frescobaldi
& R. Mondavi, "Luce",
Tuscany, 2000

Tenuta Garetto, Barbera
D'Asti, "Fava", 2000

**Pollo Parmigiana**  *pg. 102*

Ruffino, Chiant Classico
Riserva, "Ducale Gold",
1999

Torri, Chianti Colli
Senesi Riserva, 2000

Montevertine,
Il Sodaccio, 1997

**Spaghetti Bolognese** *pg. 100*

Bindella, Vino Nobile di Montepulciano, 2000

Quercetto, Chianti Classico Riserva, 1999

Bacio, "Angelica", Napa Valley, 1999

**Lasagna** *pg. 84*

Nozzole, "Il Pareto", Tuscany, 1998

Banfi, "Summus", Sant'Antimo, 1998

Marchese di Frescobaldi, "Lamaione", Tuscany, 1999

**Rigatoni Country Style** *pg. 96*

Castello di Cacchiano, Chianti Classico Riserva, 1995

R. Biale, Zinfandel, "Aldo's Vineyard", Napa Valley, 1999

Girard, Cabernet Franc, Napa Valley, 2001

**Osso Bucco di Agnello** *pg. 92*

Villa Alta, Amarone della Valpolicella Classico, 1997

Tatachilla, Shiraz, "Foundation", Mclaren Vale, 1998

Chateau La Galliane, Margaux, 1998

**Cannelloni** *pg. 74*

Davinci, Chianti, 2003

Pio Cesare, Dolcetto D'Alba, 2002

Il Poggione, Rosso di Montalcino, "Estate Bottled", 2000

## STEAKS & CHOPS

*Wine Pairings*

**New York Strip Steak**  *pg. 136*

Andrew Will, Merlot, "Klipsun
Vineyard", Walla Walla, 2001

Parkers 1st Growth,
Coonawarra, 1999

Seavey, Cabernet Sauvignon,
Napa Valley, 2001

**Pepper Steak**  *pg. 138*

Rosenblum, Zinfandel, "Samsel
Vineyard", Sonoma Valley, 2000

Kongsgaard, Syrah,
Napa Valley, 2000

Las Rocas, Garnacha, "Vinas
Viejas", San Alejandro, 2001

**Crab & Lobster Cakes**  *pg. 128*

Rochioli, Sauvignon Blanc,
Russian River Valley, 2003

Keller Estate, Chardonnay,
"La Cruz Vineyard",
Sonoma Coast, 2001

David Arthur, Chardonnay,
"Reserve", Napa Valley 2002

**Beef Wellington**  *pg. 120*

Clos du Roy, "Cuvee Artur",
Fronsac, 2000

Lail, "J. Daniel Cuvee",
Napa Valley, 2001

Errazuriz, Cabernet Sauvignon,
"Don Maximiano",
Acongua Valley, 1999

**Coriander and Pepper Seared Tuna Steak**  *pg. 122*

M. Chapoutier, "Chante Alouette", Hermitage, 1998

Dumol, Pinot Noir, Russian River Valley, 2001

Green & Red, Zinfandel, "Chiles Mill", Napa Valley, 2001

**Cowboy Steak**  *pg. 126*

Richard Partridge, Cabernet Sauvignon, Napa Valley, 2001

Quilceda Creek, Cabernet Sauvignon, Washington, 2001

Ramey, "Jericho Canyon", Napa Valley, 2001

**Grilled Pork Chop**  *pg. 134*

Aragonia, "Garnacha Centenaria", Campo de Borja, 2002

Domaine du Pagau, Chateauneuf-Du-Pape, 2001

Pierre Andre, "Champlain", Gevrey-Chambertin, 2002

**Roasted Rack of Venison**  *pg. 140*

Clos Mimi, Syrah, "Shell Creek Vineyard", Paso Robles, 1997

Stag's Leap Wine Cellars, Cabernet Sauvignon, "Artemis", Napa Valley, 1999

Michel-Schlumberger, Cabernet Sauvignon, "Reserve", Dry Creek Valley, 1999

**Ashton V.S.G.**

Bellicoso #1   5¼ x 52

Wrapper: Ecuador
Binder: Dominican Republic
Filler: Dominican Republic
Drink: Krug NV Champagne
Description: Full bodied, strong, pepper, clove

## CIGARS

If you're in search of the perfect cigar to top off your meal, check out our selections. Our handmade cigar recommendations offer the trademark of a fine cigar, consistent quality tobacco and quality construction.

### Arturo Fuente

Opus X

Wrapper: Dominican Republic
Binder: Dominican Republic
Filler: Dominican Republic
Drink: Bowmore 30-year Islay
Description: Pungant, full, spicy

### Montecristo

#2   6 x 50

Wrapper: Connecticut Shade
Binder: Dominican Republic
Filler: Dominican Republic
Drink: McCallan 18-year Speyside
Description: Medium body, slow
burning, mild spice, smooth

### Onyx Reserve

Mini Belicoso   5 x 52

Wrapper: Connecticut Shade
Binder: Nicaragua
Filler: Dominican/Nicaragua/Peru
Drink: Pierre Ferrand Selec
Des Agnes
Description: Nutmeg, orange peel,
leather

### Padron 1964 Anniversary Series

Diplomatico   7 x 50

Wrapper: Nicaragua
Binder: Nicaragua
Filler: Nicaragua
Drink: 1977 Dow's Vintage Port
Description: Sweet vanilla and
cocoa, full bodied, smooth
and soft

### Romeo Y Julieta

Vintage #11   6 x 46

Wrapper: Ecuador
Binder: Mexico
Filler: Dominican Republic
Drink: Campbell's "Rutherglen"
Muscat 1999
Description: Mild, lighter bodied,
hints of spice, smooth

### Diamond Crown

No. 2   7½ x 54

Wrapper: Connecticut Shade
Binder: Dominican Republic
Filler: Dominican Republic
Drink: Hine "Antique"
Description: Almond, oak and
orange peel, silky

## Cohiba

Triangula   6 x 54

Wrapper: Cameroon
Binder: Indonesian
Filler: Dominican Republic
Drink: Glenfarclas 21-year Speyside
Description: Ultimate in smooth, complex, even burning

## La Gloria Cubana

Series R #4   4⅞ x 52

Wrapper: Ecuador
Binder: Nicaragua
Filler: Dominican Republic
Drink: Warres 1987 Colheita
Description: Medium bodied, very smooth, hints of cedar

## La Aurora Preferidos

Perfecto   5½ x 54

Wrapper: Cameroon
Binder: Dominican Republic
Filler: Dominican Republic
Drink: Sandeman's Tawny Port
Description: Creamy, cedar, cocoa bean, consistant burn

# FISH & SEAFOOD

## Selecting Fresh Fish

Ask your fishmonger to allow you to sniff the fillets you
are buying. Remember, *fresh fish does not smell!*
If there is a fishy odor, you are smelling bacteria build
up and you should not buy that fish. It will *not* improve
with age, with washing off or with lemon juice, and it
will smell up your kitchen. Note: some seafoods will
have the sweet smell of the ocean but you should never
buy fish that smell fishy, yeasty or worse, ammoniated.

There are many different types of fish, each with their
own distinct characteristics, so we have provided a
few guidelines for purchasing the most popular species.

**Whitefish fillets:** (cod, haddock, flounder, halibut, ocean
catfish, cusk, hake): Fillets should be a natural creamy
white shade with no yellow or brown edges. Avoid fillets
that look overly bright, shiny white or as if they have
a film on them. This is evidence of chemical brining.
Fillets should have no gaping holes or tears.

**Tuna:** Tuna should be red to burgundy red. Brown tuna
is old tuna. Many times tuna steaks are wrapped in
plastic to protect them from the air — this is a good
practice.

**Swordfish:** Look for a bright red bloodline and flesh
that is translucent. Occasionally a "cherry" sword
will appear. This pinkish-orange hue is normal —
we believe it to be related to the fish's diet. A brown
bloodline or brown/grey flesh is a "no sale!"

**Scallops:** The natural color of scallops ranges from
creamy to light tan to pale orange. A uniform white
color is evidence of the industry-wide practice of
soaking scallops in sodium tripolyphosphate to mask
age and add water weight. Soaked scallops lack flavor,
have a jelly consistency and will not brown effectively.

**Shellfish:** Mussels may gape slightly but should close
when cupped in one's hand. Other shellfish such as
hardshell clams and oysters should be closed when
purchased. Discard any dead (open) shellfish before
cooking.

**Dark-meated fillets:** Dark meated fillets should look
moist and not dried out or brown. Don't be afraid of
dark meated fillets such as Mahi Mahi or Pollock,
they cook up light and flaky.

## Storing Fish at Home

It is always best to prepare fish within 1–2 days of purchase because a home refrigerator is not cold enough
to effectively preserve "just caught" flavor for longer
than 48 hours. Here are a few tips for home storage:

**In the Refrigerator** Remember keeping fish cold is the
key to keeping it delicious. Take fish directly home from
the store. Unwrap the packaging and place fish in a
glass pyrex dish with cover. Store fish in the coldest
portion of your refrigerator—typically the back corner
away from the door. Do not freeze fish that is past its
prime, it will not improve in your home freezer.

**In the Freezer** Freeze fish the day you purchase it.
Wrap it in plastic wrap and place into a Ziploc freezer
bag, expelling all the air as you close the bag. If you
have a large quantity of fish to freeze, separate it into
several packages or it will freeze too slowly to maintain
quality. Keep fish no longer than 1 month. Your home
freezer is not cold enough to completely retard the bacteria growth which impairs flavor and causes spoilage.

## Preparing Fish at Home

**The Golden Rule:** Fish is best when cooked at high heat
for a short amount of time. This seals in flavor without
drying out fillets. One simple rule covers it all: Cook
fish at 450 degrees for 10 minutes per inch of thickness. Meatier fish such as swordfish may take slightly
longer. When cooking fillets turn tail portion under to
get even thickness and ensure even cooking.

**Don't Rinse:** Do not rinse fish before cooking. Rinsing
washes away water soluable proteins that give fish its
delicious flavor.

**Doneness:** We believe the optimum cooking doneness
for seafood is medium-rare. At this state of doneness,
whitefish will flake easily yet retain its natural glistening moisture. Tuna will retain a pink core and the center
of scallops will be just lukewarm to the touch. If you
prefer fish cooked to medium doneness, just add a
couple minutes to cooking time. Do not overcook.

## Cooking Methods

**Sauté:** It is critical when sautéing seafood to preheat the pan before adding oil or butter. Also, do not overcrowd the pan as the fish will not brown properly. Almost any fish can be sautéed with delicious results. For scallops and flounder, it is the preferred cooking method.

**Deep Fry:** When deep frying be sure the oil is at the proper temperature before adding the fish—we keep a candy thermometer for testing the oil and find that 375 degrees works well for most fish. Deep frying locks in moisture and is a great preparation method for many fish and shellfish including oysters, squid, scallops, flounder, haddock and pollock.

**Bake:** The key to success in baking fish is to have your oven preheated. Remember the golden rule: cook fish at 450 degrees for 10 minutes per inch of thickness. We like to add a tablespoon or two of water to the baking pan to humidify the oven. Most fish lend themselves to baking but because of the thinness of flounder fillets, we recommend that they be rolled if they are to be baked.

**Grill:** Oil grill racks and preheat the grill before starting the fish. Follow the golden rule of baked fish—10 minutes per inch of thickness. To enhance your presentation with criss-cross grill marks, start fish in one direction then after 2 to 3 minutes, rotate the fish 90 degrees. The best grillfish are: swordfish, striped bass, tuna, salmon, monkfish and any fillet when put in foil.

Real Seafood Co., Toledo

# PASTA

The mere word conjures up images of heaping, steaming bowls of multi-colored, multi-shaped pasta preparations. To an Italian, there is nothing more appetizing or more tempting than a bowl of freshly cooked pasta, shining with green oil or luscious butter, topped with vegetables or fish or meat sauces, and sprinkled with incomparable cheeses.

Pasta is synonymous with Italy - colorful, ebullient, and gregarious in the South and refined, restrained and more complex in the North. Pasta is the food of peasants and kings alike and it is, undoubtedly, one of Italy's greatest culinary assets.

The image of pasta in this country has changed considerably in the last few years. It is now fashionable and chic to make your own pasta and to order it in a restaurant. This ancient Italian staple, whose origins are still disputed, has become a favorite of American chefs.

Homemade or factory-made pasta begins by working flour and eggs, or flour and water, into a dough. This dough is then kneaded and rolled out for the homemade product, or it is put through the extruders of large commercial pasta machines to form various shapes for the factory-made.

## Pasta and Its Sauces

In all my years of cooking, I have never thought about matching the pasta with the sauce. I know that traditionally, the tagliatelle or bologna are served with Bolognese meat sauce (but not always) and the Roman fettuccine with ragu alla romana or with a butter and cheese sauce. I know that with pappardelle, the largest of all noodles, a nice assertive meat or game sauce is in order and that linguine and spaghetti are the perfect vehicles for shellfish. I also know that with the colorful and zesty sauces of Southern Italy, a stubby cut of pasta such as rigatoni, bucatini, or fusilli is demanded. But, matching the pasta with sauce...really!

On second thought, how about the orecchiette with broccoli or Puglia? And the Spaghetti alla Chitarra with lamb sauce of Abruzzo? Now, I am all confused and probably so are you!

Yes, there are many sauces in Italy that traditionally belong to specific types of pasta shapes and the explanation for all this would probably fill a small book. So, in order to simplify this topic, I will make a few simple suggestions.

**Spaghetti and linguine** are the perfect vehicles for fish and shellfish sauces.

**Angel hair and taglioline,** traditionally served in clear broth, also can be served with light butter-cream sauces or with fresh tomato sauce.

**Wide noodles and large macaroni** pair well with meat and game sauces.

**Factory made pasta** such as penne, ziti, bucatini, spaghetti, etc; are perfect for the bold oil-based sauces of Southern Italy.

**Orecchiette penne, shells and rotelle** are great with vegetable sauces and tomato sauces.

**Fettuccine and tagliatelle** are succulent with butter, cream and cheese sauces but also with meat sauces and with tomato-cream prosciutto or panacea sauces.

**Cannelloni** is one those delightful mysteries in food. It has a huge flavor and can be quite filling, but at the same time, it's extremely light, chewing is almost optional. Like good wine, you can swirl it around in your mouth before it melts down to your throat. So what makes cannelloni so different from any of the other pasta dishes? First it's made with Italian meats like prosciutto and mortadella for flavor impact. Second, both the pasta and filling are intended to be very thin. When it's rolled up, it's on many layers, like puff pastry and croissant, multiple thin layers produce a very tender dish. Finally, cannelloni is baked in béchamel made with milk, butter and flour. Fresh pasta, a flavorful filling, and simple cream sauce. What's not to love!

If this is still too confusing to you, keep in mind the following:

Use full-bodied pasta with full-bodied sauces.

Use light, delicate pastas with delicate sauce.

But most of all, find the combination that works for you and simply enjoy it!

## Some Golden Rules for Perfectly Cooked and Perfectly Sauced Pasta

**Always use a large pot with plenty of water.** For one pound of pasta, you will need approximately four to five quarts of water.

**When the water boils**, add the salt and the pasta all at once. Cover the pot and bring water back to boil, then remove the lid. The salt will season the pasta thoroughly and lightly, highlighting its wholesome, unique character.

**Stir pasta** a few times as it cooks. If you have plenty of water in the pot and you give it an occasional stir, the pasta will not stick together. Adding oil to the water is unnecessary and not advisable for it will make the pasta slippery.

**The cooking time** of pasta will depend on the size, the type and the shape of the pasta. The fresher and thinner the pasta, the shorter the cooking time. Freshly made pasta will cook in no time at all. The longer it dries, the longer it needs to cook. Fresh, homemade noodles will cook faster than fresh homemade stuffed pasta since stuffed pasta has double the thickness.

**The cooking of factory-made pasta** also depends on the shape, thickness and brand of the pasta. To be safe, read the cooking instructions on the package but taste the pasta for doneness often during cooking.

**Perfectly cooked pasta** should be tender but still firm to bite, al dente. To an Italian, there is no greater sin than overcooked pasta. Keep in mind that pasta keeps cooking even after it has been drained.

**Once pasta is cooked**, drain it, then transfer it to a warm bowl and toss it immediately with sauce (this can be done in a large, warm bowl or in the skillet where the sauce is kept simmering).

**Never add all the sauce at once**, you might not need it or want it all. Start with half the amount and add more if you like it. Keep in mind that pasta served the Italian way is never over sauced.

**If adding pasta to the simmering sauce** in the skillet, make sure to under-cook your pasta a bit more than usual so it can be tossed together with the sauce over the heat briefly. By doing this, you will achieve two things. The pasta will be piping hot when it's served and it will be thoroughly coated with the hot sauce (this is an old restaurant trick).

**Remember** that pasta does not wait for anyone, so serve it at once, making sure that everyone is already sitting in anticipation at the table.

# TOMATOES

Tomatoes reached Italy at the end of the 16th century, but only appeared on the culinary scene many years later when a new strain was developed from seeds brought to Italy from Mexico by two Jesuits. They grew well in Southern Italy and, in the 18th century, began to be added to traditional country dishes both for their flavor and their color.

It was in Naples that tomatoes found their new homeland and the Neapolitans were quick enough to see the great potential of this new fruit. Tomatoes went on to conquer the rest of Italy during the 19th century.

It was in 1875, that tomatoes were first cultivated for processing when the first concentrate was made in the province of Parma, and by 1900, this was an industry of some considerable size. In the South, at about the same time, the canning of peeled tomatoes started. Since then, the cultivation, processing, and canning of tomatoes, mostly based in Campania, has become one of Italy's largest agricultural based industries. The best tomatoes for canning and cooking are the San Marzano plum tomatoes, a great point in their favor being that they all ripen at more or less the same time and peel easily.

Tomatoes can be preserved at home either whole or in a cooked sauce, which I think is easier. To preserve them whole, they need to be peeled and placed in hermetically sealed jars which are sterilized for about one hour per pound. In Southern Italy, they are preserved the natural way, given the hot, dry climate, dried in the sun. They are then kept through the winter, hanging from the kitchen ceiling.

The other way to have good tomato flavoring in store for winter is to make a plain sauce, flavored only with a little garlic and herbs and then either sterilize it in hermetically sealed jars or freeze it.

In villages through central and southern Italy, the winter stock of tomato sauce is prepared all in one day by the entire village.

The uses of tomatoes in Italian cooking are endless. They are made into sauces to dress pasta, gnocchi and pizza. They are added to other food for flavoring, they are eaten in salads, and stewed with other vegetables.

One final word. When you make tomato sauce with canned tomatoes, cook it enough for the water to evaporate and flavor to concentrate. I add a teaspoon of sugar and a little concentrated tomato paste for more flavor.

Zia's, Toledo

# OLIVE OIL

Olive oil is the ingredient that unites all Italian cooking. Even though butter is widely used in the North, olive oil has its own special place and its usage is increasing by leaps and bounds. The reason? Olive oil is very good and it's also very good for us.

Of course olive oil is the cooking fat of Central and Southern Italy because of the abundance of olive trees spread throughout the landscape.

The best, most popular, and most expensive oil is extra virgin olive oil. This oil is produced without chemical means, by stone crushing and cold pressing hand picked olives. It also has the lowest acidity, under one percent.

Virgin olive oil is produced in the same manner, using riper olives which have fallen to the ground. This oil has a higher degree of acidity which can be up to, but not more than, four percent.

Pure olive oil is, in spite of its label, the most common oil. It is rectified (deodorized, deacidified, and decolorized by chemical means). Many brands available in supermarkets fall in the category of pure olive oil.

Italy has a wide range of extra virgin olive oils, from deep green and strongly flavored oil of Sicilia to the light, golden oil of Liguria and the Veneto, and, in between, there are the great oils of Toscana, Umbria and Puglia. Fortunately, today we can find Italian olive oils, not only at our specialized markets, but, quite often at our local supermarkets. Try several brands and settle on the one you prefer.

Extra virgin olive oil has a place of prominence in my home pantry and in my restaurant. Use extra virgin olive oil whenever you can obtain it or can afford it. A few drops of fragrant green extra virgin olive oil can go quite far and give your cooking the unmistakable Italian taste.

**Storing Olive Oil** Olive oil can be kept quite well for many months provided you store it in the coolest, darkest part of your pantry in a tightly closed bottle (do not store it in plastic). Olive oil does not need to be refrigerated.

**Oil for frying**. Many Italians use a pure olive oil for frying. My preference, however, is a more neutrally flavored oil, such as corn or peanut oil.

# CHEESES

## Parmigiano-Reggiano

It is hard to imagine Italian cooking without parmigiano-reggiano. This noble cheese, produced under strict regulations in the provinces of Parma, Reggio, Modena, Mantua and Bolgna is made with milk produced between the first of April and the eleventh of November. Twelve hundred cheese-making dairies produce this superlative cheese which is made by hand by artisan cheese makers following a tradition that has remained unchanged for seven centuries.

When buying parmigiano, look for the word "Parmigiano-Reggiano" etched in tiny dots on the rind of the cheese. By law, parmigiano-reggiano is aged at least one year. Sometimes in this country, we find a two year old parmigiano which is exceptionally good. Good parmigiano should have a straw yellow color with a crumbly but moist texture.

Parmigiano is an expensive cheese but a little goes a long way. A nice chunk of parmigiano can be wrapped in plastic and kept in the refrigerator for two to three weeks without losing any of its freshness. If the cheese dries out a bit, wrap it in a damp cloth and leave it in the refrigerator for a few hours, then remove the cloth and wrap the cheese again in plastic.

## Grana Padana

Grana padana is an excellent cheese, similar to parmigiano-reggiano, but is produced outside the restricted area that produces parmigiano. Grana padana is perhaps the only acceptable substitute for parmigiano.

## Mozzarella

Mozzarella is a very popular cheese essential to many Southern Italian preparations. The most prized mozzarella in Italy is made from the curd of water buffalo milk. Unfortunately, the number of domesticated water buffalo in Southern Italy is rapidly shrinking in number and it is getting harder to find real mozzarella di buffalo. What we often find today is mozzarella prepared with a percentage of buffalo milk and a percentage of cow's milk. This is still an extremely delicious cheese and can be found imported from Italy in Italian markets and specialty food stores across the country. If you are lucky enough to find some good mozzarella imported from Italy, buy more than you need and freeze what you don't use right away (freezing mozzarella is unanimously approved by the cheese makers of Southern Italy). Thaw the mozzarella overnight in the refrigerator.

Cow's milk mozzarella is also quite popular in Italy. In the United States, good locally made cow's milk mozzarella, such as Polly-O's whole milk Fior di Latte, can be found in Italian neighborhoods and specialty stores. The factory-made mozzarella found on the supermarket shelves is tough and rubbery and has no relation to the real thing.

Smoked mozzarella is also available. Remember, when seasoning, smoked mozzarella is quite salty.

## Ricotta

Ricotta is a cheese by-product made from the watery part of the cow's milk. This soft, delicious cheese is used in the filling for many pasta preparations and in the ricotta cakes and pastries of the South. Since ricotta is quite perishable, it is not often available imported from Italy. However, just like mozzarella, good fresh ricotta can often be found in Italian markets and specialty stores. The whole milk ricotta available in supermarkets is an acceptable substitute.

## Gorgonzola

Gorgonzola is a soft, blue-veined table cheese made from cow's milk. This buttery cheese was originally produced in the small village of Gorgonzola, near Milano, and aged in rocky caves. Today, however, this delicious cheese is produced in specially designed areas of Piedmont of Lombardia.

While a mature gorgonzola, aged five to six months, has a pungent, direct taste, a two to three month old gorgonzola is milder and sweeter. Even though gorgonzola is a delicious table cheese, often served with grapes, pears and nuts, it shines when it becomes a component in a creamy, delicate pasta sauce.

## Fontina

Fontina is another great table cheese. This tender, mild, cow's milk cheese produced in Val d' Aosta dates back to the Middle Ages. Because of its soft, melting quality, fontina cheese is frequently used for cooking.

## Pecorino

Pecorino cheese is made from sheep's milk. There are many varieties of pecorino cheese and they vary greatly, depending on the area where they are made. The best known pecorino in this country is pecorino romano, a sharp, strong, assertive hard cheese, mainly used as a grating cheese in Roman and Southern Italian preparations.

There are, however, other pecorino cheeses which are milder and are generally used as table cheeses. My personal preferences are the pecorinos made in Toscana and Umbria, which are mild and tender, with just a bit of peppery bite to them.

## Mascarpone

Mascarpone is a double cream cheese that originated in Lombardia. The heavy cream is coagulated by the addition of citric acid which gives this cheese its characteristically slightly sour taste. Mascarpone cheese is high in butter fat and has a thick, heavy consistency that resembles that of sour cream. This delicious cheese is used primarily in delicate pasta dishes and desserts and is the essential ingredient in the famous Italian dessert tiramisu (cream cheese is not an acceptable substitute for mascarpone).

# HERBS

Herbs, just like garlic, should be used in moderation. Somehow we have this image of Italian food loaded with all kinds of herbs. A bit of fresh sage added to boiled potatoes will give a decisive delicious touch. Too much will be quite overpowering. A little chopped fresh rosemary added to stewed game will bring out he flavor of the meat. Too much will give the sauce a bitter taste. If fresh herbs are not available, we must use dried herbs, also with moderation, for some might be too assertive and others might lack their original aroma. Our good common sense should tell us to always start with a little for we can always add more.

**Parsley**, just like olive oil and parmigiano, is a basic Italian ingredient. The parsley used in Italy, however, is not the curly type most commonly available in supermarkets but the flat, broad-leveled parsley, also called appropriately "Italian Parsley". It has a sweet fragrant flavor which enhances the taste of innumerable dishes. Today, Italian parsley is quite often available in supermarkets.

**Basil** is one of the most popular herbs with its sweet taste and pretty green laves and the fact that it embodies the spirit of summer. We use it in the ever popular pesto sauce, in salads, and over pasta. In Italy, even the most modest cook has a little pot with basil on her window. This is one of those herbs that I do not bother to use unless it's fresh.

**Rosemary** is a wonderful aromatic herb is used extensively throughout Italy, especially, in conjunction with grilled or roasted meat and fowl. Dried rosemary, if used in moderation, is quite acceptable.

**Sage** is more popular in the northern part of Italy, where it is properly paired with game cooking, then it is in the south. I also love sage in savory breads and roasted potatoes as well as in marinades. Use dried sage leaves judiciously because they can be quite overpowering.

**Oregano** is mild and sweet and gently aromatic. It appears in many southern Italian dishes, either fresh or dried, especially in the many appetizing tomato sauce. Again, use dried oregano only in moderation.

# COOKING WINES & VINEGARS

## Cooking Wines

**White**: In Italian home cooking, most sauces are products from a reduction of pan juices added to some wine, broth or cream. Therefore, the quality of the liquid we use to produce a sauce is important. Don't choose a ninety-cent bottle of wine for cooking. Choose a wine that you would enjoy drinking, then use a bit of that for your sauce. Of course, if a wine is expensive, you probably would rather drink it than cook with it. But, if you think of wine as an important ingredient which will affect the quality of your dish, perhaps you don't mind using a cup of good wine for your sauce.

**Marsala**: A bit of good Marsala can transform an ordinary dish into a delicacy. This wonderful aromatic wine comes from Marsala in Sicilica. Most people know how delicious a few slices of veal are when they are tossed with a bit of Marsala, but this wine can be used for so many other preparations. A veal, pork, or turkey roast, for example, will become irresistible with the addition of some Marsala. A bit of Marsala will enrich the sauce of a stew and many desserts would not taste the same without it. Marsala comes sweet and dry. Use dry Marsala for cooking and sweet Marsala for desserts and pastries. Look for imported Marsala, such as Florio and Pellegrino, which is available in Italian markets and wine shops. Domestic Marsala is not an acceptable substitute.

## Balsamic Vinegar

Balsamic vinegar is an aromatic, concentrated product made from the boiled down must of white Trebbiano grapes and it is a specialty of Modena, a lovely city in Emilia-Romagna. In the sixteenth century, this vinegar was considered so precious that it was often made part of a legacy in a will and given as a dowry. The production of real balsamic vinegar takes many decades. The boiled-down must of grapes is aged from many years in a series of barrels, moving the contents of the barrel to another of diminishing size and wood after much of the vinegar has evaporated, all of which gives a different fragrance to the vinegar. This process is repeated approximately every ten years until the vinegar has acquired that special thick, velvety, high aromatic quality that defines it.

In Modena, seventy or eighty year old vinegar can still be found among some families which have been making it for generations or, with luck, one can obtain it from some of the few remaining artisans who still make it for sale (years ago, I had the good fortune to savor a thirty-year-old vinegar and I thought I had died and gone to heaven). Today, most balsamic vinegar available is commercially produced and aged two, three, or five years. I suppose we should be grateful for little miracles because, even though this product is light years away from wonderful homemade product, it is still reasonably pleasant. Sometimes in this country, you can find a ten, fifteen, or twenty year old vinegar. If you can afford it, but use it sparingly and wisely, keeping in mind that you will need only a few drops to enrich a dish. Balsamic vinegar should read Aceto balsamico tradizionale di Modena or Reggio Emilio.

## Vinegar

In Italian home cooking, vinegar is used far beyond the regular salad. A few drops of good red wine vinegar can be added to a fish stew, to game and to liver. Vinegar is also the essential element in many sweet and sour dishes. Choose a wine vinegar that has a deep red color and that is free of other seasoning such as garlic and herbs. White wine vinegar is occasionally used.

# LOCATIONS

*For reservations*
*1-888-456-DINE*

**Corporate Offices**
Mainstreet Ventures, Inc.
605 South Main Street, Suite 2
Ann Arbor, Michigan 48104

*www.msventures.com*

## Michigan

**Real Seafood Company**
341 South Main Street
Ann Arbor, Michigan 48104

**Palio Ristorante**
347 South Main Street
Ann Arbor, Michigan 48104

**Gratzi Ristorante**
326 South Main Street
Ann Arbor, Michigan 48104

**The Chop House & La Dolce Vita**
322 South Main Street
Ann Arbor, Michigan 48104

**Carson's American Bistro**
2000 Commonwealth Blvd.,
off Plymouth Road
Ann Arbor, Michigan 48105

**The Chop House**
190 Monroe Ave NW
Grand Rapids, Michigan 49503

## Ohio

**Real Seafood Company**
The Docks Restaurants
22 Main Street
Toledo, Ohio 43605

**Zia's**
The Docks Restaurants
20 Main Street
Toledo, Ohio 43605

**Ciao**
6064 Monroe Street
Sylvania, Ohio 43560

**Carson's American Bistro**
5839 Monroe Street
Sylvania, Ohio 43560
(opening fall 2005)

## West Virginia

**Tidewater Grill**
1060 Charleston Town Center
Charleston, West Virginia 25389

**Gratzi**
1061 Charleston Town Center
Charleston, West Virginia 25389

**The Chop House**
1003 Charleston Town Center
Charleston, West Virginia 25389

## Florida

**Blue Pointe**
13499 SE Cleveland Ave #141
Fort Myers, Florida 33907

**Real Seafood Compnay**
8960 Fontana Del Solway #103
Naples, Florida 34109

**Carson's American Bistro**
18767 S. Tamiami Trail
Ft. Myers, Florida 33908

# INDEX